Dunkirk
A Personal Memoir

This book is dedicated to
my dear wife Anne
who encouraged me to write it
but died before she was able
to read it

Dunkirk
A Personal Memoir

A Year in the Life of a
Territorial Army Recruit
1939–1940

Ralph W. Wild

MERTON

First published 2004

Published by
Merton Priory Press Ltd
67 Merthyr Road, Whitchurch
Cardiff CF14 1DD

ISBN 1 898937 62 1

Printed by
Dinefwr Press
Rawlings Road, Llandybie
Carmarthenshire SA18 3YD

Contents

List of Illustrations

Introduction

In 2000, on the sixtieth anniversary of the Dunkirk evacuation, what happened then was much in the public mind. I was there and was rescued from the beach on the night before the final night of the operation. My experience was quite different from what most people thought had happened. This even applied to commentators on television and in the newspapers. There seemed to be a general picture of a disorganised mass of troops on the beaches who were taken off by small boats from the Thames and South Coast harbours and transported by them across the Channel. Some even thought that there had been hand-to-hand fighting with the Germans on the beach itself.

In fact the 'Little Ships', as they came to be called, did a valiant, self-sacrificing job assisting the Royal Navy by ferrying men out from the shallow waters of the beaches to the naval and civilian ships waiting off-shore. A substantial number of troops embarked directly from the harbour or breakwater. The Germans did not reach the beaches during the operation because, until the very last day, the BEF's rearguard held the German advance on the Belgian side of the border some ten miles from Dunkirk at the nearest point. At the same time the French halted the German forces in the west after the enemy had taken Gravelines.

These false pictures can probably be ascribed to the books written by men who had somehow got separated from their units, whose description of their adventures got made into films. The film-makers have understandably emphasised the more dramatic aspects of the story they have to tell, but people do not realise that this was a small part of the larger scene.

A historian speaking recently on BBC radio pointed out that as the generations died out, knowledge of how people lived in their times was lost unless they had recorded their memories. At the age of ninety, therefore, I have decided to write down what I remember of the most momentous year of my life.

My memories of the BEF campaign consist of a series of mind pictures, in which I see events in vivid detail. These I have attempted to put into words. I have consulted Norman Gelb's book *Dunkirk*, to check my dates. This gives a comprehensive description of Operation Dynamo and of the political comings and goings at the time, and I have obtained official figures of casualties in the services from it. I have also re-read *Return Via Dunkirk* by 'Gunbuster', a pseudonym for an officer in one of our batteries. This is almost entirely concerned with the experiences of his own battery. Some of the events he recorded I have recounted also. Where my account differs from his, it is because I have faith in my own recollections. I have quoted from this book details showing how different were the living conditions of officers from those of junior rank, even in action. Otherwise I have recorded nothing except what I remember of events at which I was present or of which I had immediate knowledge.

I am indebted to Remember When, the South Croydon Newspaper Archive, for locating the headline in the *Sunday Express* printed on page 12. I am also grateful to my daughter Amanda for help in preparing the maps and illustrations for the book, and to my son Martin, who proof-read it for me.

In the accounts of Dunkirk, little mention has been made of the part played by Territorial Army units. The 50th Division, to which my regiment was attached for the duration of the fighting, was a Territorial division—the Tyneside Terriers. Our own division—the 5th, was Regular, but one of the other artillery regiments was also Territorial. These two divisions formed Frankforce, which was part of the Army's rearguard from the time that it was decided that Operation Dynamo should be attempted. As a tribute to the Territorial Army I have written this book in the form of the autobiography of a recruit who joined in May 1939, of how he was assimilated into the military machine and saw action a year later, of the journey from a desk in County Hall to the beaches of Dunkirk.

Sunday, 2 June 1940

… As our train drew into Tonbridge station, we saw that the platform was full of women and girls in bright summer dresses waving and calling their greetings. When the train stopped, they handed through the open windows tea and lemonade, sweets, cigarettes and cakes … Just before the train drew out, bundles of Sunday newspapers arrived. The one I got was the *Sunday Express*. Across the front page was the banner headline:

Last Night's Ordeal of the Last Thin Line of Dunkirk

'Hell!', I said, 'Our people at home must be worried about us …'

1 The author and his wife Anne after their marriage in December 1940.

PART ONE : TRAINING

1

May 1939

By the spring of 1939 it seemed that war was inevitable. Anne, my fiancée, and I both worked at County Hall in London. For months she had worked overtime typing schedules for the evacuation of schoolchildren and mothers with children under five. She had been appointed to help shepherd a tram-load of the latter to a local station and thence to an unknown destination on the day appointed for their evacuation. I was suddenly told that I was to do an office job in the Heavy Rescue Service, which my department was organising and that I would be 'reserved' from call-up. This was something which could be done equally well by a woman or older man. I therefore applied for permission, which I knew could not be refused, to join the Territorial Army. This came through the same day.

That evening, on my way home, I alighted from my bus half-way along Kennington Road where there was a notice-board pointing towards the Regimental Headquarters of a Territorial unit—the 92nd Army Field Regiment, R.A., T.A. I went down the side street indicated and found myself in a drill-yard packed with men. After a short while a small man with a large voice, who I later discovered was the Regimental Sergeant Major, emerged from a temporary building on the far side of the yard and stood on the steps leading up to the door. He announced that recruitment to the regiment was almost complete and that only drivers and surveyors were required. 'Unless you have either a driving licence or a matric certificate', he said, 'you may like to go round the corner to Braganza Street, where the Queen's Regiment is still recruiting'. Most of the crowd departed and those of us who were left queued up outside the office door.

We went through the process of enlistment in threes. Each of us filled in a form then took oath of allegiance to the King. For this purpose it was necessary for the sergeant dealing with us to way-lay one of the officers rushing in and out of an inner office. When one of them was finally seated at the table opposite us, he demanded, 'Where's that bloody Bible?' I realised I was entering an environment with which I was not familiar. We three recited the oath in unison, signed a paper, the officer shook each of us by the hand and fled once more into his office. We were in the Army.

I found that I was to be a surveyor in 365 Battery. We were told to attend a drill night the following week and where to report. The RSM told me I was to come to the regimental office. The battery could not start training surveyors just yet but that the permanent staff needed clerical help.

So my 'drill' nights were spent doing clerical work. It was undemanding—not what I had in mind when I enlisted, but the permanent staff were obviously overwhelmed by the amount of paperwork involved in the expansion of the Territorial Army. I was issued my uniform, battledress, which was replacing the service dress previously worn. At the beginning of August the regiment went (with, I understood, the rest of the TA in the London District) to its training camp. This took place at Beaulieu Heath in Hampshire and lasted for two weeks. I thought that now I might at last go to my Battery and start my training as a surveyor. When we arrived, however, the RSM told me I was to continue to do clerical work at Regimental Headquarters. He had a special job for me. So I spent the whole fortnight in the marquee, which had been designated as RHQ. The 'special job' was to complete hundreds of multi-page forms—one for each member of the regiment. On these had to be entered details of attendance at drill nights, for which a bounty was paid, weekend and other training, including the annual camp, for which each man was paid, at army rates.

In the event, I was better off sitting in the marquee doing this routine work than if I had gone to my Battery, for during the

```
                                    Army Form E 654
                                      (Pads of 50.)
TERRITORIAL ARMY or SUPPLEMENTARY RESERVE.

NOTICE TO JOIN FOR TRAINING IN CAMP.

Name    R. W. Wild
Number  901457        365/92nd  Field  Regiment
            YOU ARE HEREBY DIRECTED to attend at

                   Kennington
on            30 JUL 1939        19      at not later
than       9        o'clock a.m.    H.W. Westlake
                                        Adjutant.
Date 24 JUL 1939
```

LEAVE OF ABSENCE from Annual Training in Camp can only be granted for *most urgent reasons.* Any applications for such leave must be received by the O.C. by...............(date). Men absent without leave are hereby warned that they are liable to be proceeded against in the civil courts.

INSURANCE CARDS AND UNEMPLOYMENT BOOKS.—If you are insured under the National Health Insurance Acts, and Widows' Orphans' and Old Age Contributory Pensions Acts, immediately before training, you are required to bring your insurance card with you when joining for the annual training as directed above. You should also bring your unemployment book with you if you normally belong to an insured employment under the Unemployment Insurance Acts.

2 The order to join a training camp, July 1939.

fourteen days we were at Beaulieu it rained incessantly. The vehicle and gun parks were churned up and left eighteen inches deep in mud. The ridiculous short puttees worn round the ankles with battledress proved completely impracticable and we were all thankful when they were replaced after a few months with webbing anklets.

The only thing that happened at camp which left a lasting impression on me occurred when I was walking across a field on my way to a meal. I had had no military training whatsoever, though I could stand to attention and knew how to salute from my experience in the Boys' Brigade. Coming towards me was the RSM. He was in service dress, made in the cloth used for officers' uniforms, and wore a Sam Browne belt. This completely threw me. I was pretty sure he was a warrant officer, but did the Sam Browne mean he was an officer? I decided not to risk it and popped up a salute. He affected rage, in traditional sergeant-major fashion. Did I not know I only saluted officers? I told him the Sam Browne had confused me. 'Well now you know', he said, and walked on. I had begun to learn.

The forms had to be completed before the end of camp—so that the men could be paid what was due to them at the pay parade on the last day. Consolidated accounts, however, had still to be completed, so after our return from camp I went in twice a week to help. When I arrived the following week I learned that an advance party had been called up. On the Thursday 31 August Anne let me know that she had been instructed to proceed the following day with the evacuation duties to which she had long been allocated. I was not surprised, therefore, when I entered RHQ that evening to meet one of the permanent sergeant instructors about to take a large trayful of brown envelopes to the post office. 'Are they what I think they are?', I asked. He said they were and that we were to report immediately. I went home, laid out my uniform and got my kit together.

2

1 September 1939

My call-up duly arrived in the morning post. Considering it was to transform my life it was quite a small document. It said that 365/92 Field Regt RA (T) was, on the instructions of the Army Council, to be embodied on 1 September 1939 and that 901457 Gnr. Wild, R.W. was to attend at H.Q. Kennington that day. I donned my uniform, took leave of my mother and went to County Hall. Here I told Staff Section that I was off, said farewell to some of my colleagues, took a bus to the now familiar stop in Kennington Road and reported to RHQ. I was now a full-time soldier.

I was not surprised to be told to help immediately with the paperwork involved in the members of the regiment reporting for duty. They came in throughout the day and were sent by lorry as soon as they arrived to our billeting area in Cheam, Surrey. The flow of men dried up by the early evening and the officers and permanent staff left for Cheam. Another clerk and I were issued a blanket each and given a couple of sandwiches and a mug of tea and told to remain in the office overnight in case any more men reported.

I had not been in the Army long before I began to realise how circumscribed were the circles in which I had moved hitherto. My first lesson in this respect came from the clerk with whom I was left. His name was Jimmy Bagley. He was not very tall, had very fair hair and wore gold-rimmed spectacles with very thick lenses. He came from a docker's family and had a cockney accent to match. He had, however, had a good grammar school education, was highly intelligent and had a good job in the City. The newspaper I read was the *Morning Post*, not because of its politics, which were very Right-wing, but because it had better rugby football reports than any other paper. From its reports of

No. ....   Army Form E 635.
                      Territorial Army.   (In pads of 50)

                      ## EMBODIMENT.

                      ### NOTICE TO JOIN.
No., Rank }   *901457 : Gnr. Wild , R.W.*
and Name }
                   ROYAL REGT. OF ARTILLERY.   Regt. or Corps.

    Whereas the Army Council, in pursuance of His Majesty's Proclamation, have
directed that the....*565/92 Field Regt RA (T)*...............................

be embodied on the...................-day of....**SEP 1939**....

    You are hereby required to attend at..*H.Q. Kennington.*

not later than.........................o'clock that day. Should you not present yourself as ordered
you will be liable to be proceeded against.

    You should comply with the instructions contained in your Army Book 3 (Territorial
Army Soldier's Pocket Book) regarding procedure on being called out for service, and disposal
of your National Health Insurance Card and Unemployment Book.

    If married you should complete the statement of family particulars in the pocket book
before you leave home and bring that book with you ready to be handed in when you report
for duty.

                              J.W.G. Westlake for
....
                                                          Adjutant.
Date   **4 SEP 1939**...

3 The author's call-up paper, September 1939.

events in the Docklands I had the impression that the dockers
were an unruly lot, ready to make trouble at any time and a
Communist menace. Jimmy enlightened me. He told me how
they had to gather at the dock gates every morning and afternoon. Gangers selected whom they wanted and the rest were
unlucky. If your face did not fit you got little or no work. Little
wonder that they did their best to organise themselves against
this inhumane system. The cry 'One out, all out' became
understandable and I gained respect for men like Ernest Bevin
who ultimately led the dockers to a better way of life. In spite of
his background, Jimmy was fiercely patriotic and determined to
do his bit to defeat Hitler. More of Jimmy later.

    We had to decide where to sleep. The office in which we had

worked all day was furnished with some trestle tables and folding chairs. We investigated the room used by the officers. The furniture here was similarly sparse. The floor was very dusty. We decided to use a trestle table each as a bed. We folded our battledress blouses as pillows, took off our boots, wrapped ourselves in our blankets and tried to sleep. It was not a comfortable introduction to active service, but we were to experience worse before very long.

Early the following morning a vehicle came for us. As I boarded the lorry I reflected ruefully that today Anne and I should have been travelling to Swanage. Ours was not the only holiday to be cancelled that summer. On arrival at Cheam we were sent to the house where we were to be billeted.

This proved to be grand in our eyes. The door was opened by a very smart maid. She said we were expected and she showed us to our room. Our hosts, she said, were a Mr and Mrs Umney. We deposited our kits, had a wash and shave and went downstairs. The maid, whose name we found was Mary, gave us breakfast in the kitchen where she said Mrs Umney thought we might like to take our meals. This suited us down to the ground. She told us that Mr Umney owned the firm which made Wright's coal tar soap and that he and wife were nice people. This we found to be more than true.

We went back to Regimental Headquarters, which was housed in a semi-detached house on a new estate. Jimmy was a clerk in the Regimental Quartermaster's office and I was told I was to help out there too. This was situated in the house next door. There we found the Quartermaster Sergeant and the sergeant in charge of technical stores. They were busy and we were put to work straight away.

The next morning we crowded into a room where there was a wireless set to hear the Prime Minister, Neville Chamberlain, address the nation. He announced that Germany had failed to answer our ultimatum to stop the invasion of Poland and that we were therefore at war. This pronouncement was received in an atmosphere of inevitability. We were not thrilled. Several of us had been born during the 1914–18 war and all had been brought up in its aftermath. We knew what our fathers' generation had endured in the trenches of Flanders. This war was a job to be got through. Hitler had to be defeated and the world made a safe place once more. Shortly after the broadcast finished, the air raid siren sounded. Everyone scanned the clear blue sky for the Luftwaffe to appear, but nothing happened. The 'All Clear' sounded and we went back to work.

Work in the quartermaster's stores was hard. I was introduced to Army Form G1098, a document which set out for each unit, in great detail, its personnel, armament and equipment on being mobilised. Crates and boxes were delivered day after day. The contents had to be identified, checked against the G1098 and distributed to the Batteries. We worked for ten hours a day and were glad at last to repair to the comfort of our billet. There, we were fed very well. Mary asked us if we would like some beer with our dinner. Naturally we said we would and each day a bottle of Pilsner lager appeared beside each plate. After a couple of weeks Mary said that Mrs Umney was sorry but they could no longer get Pilsner lager as it from Czechoslovakia. Would pale ale do instead? This was typical of the kindness which we were treated.

A few days after we were called up we were ordered to undergo a medical examination the next day. Jimmy was in a panic. He confessed to me that he was virtually blind in one eye and it was obvious from the thickness of the lenses in his spectacles that the other was not good either. Furthermore, he said, he had a double hernia which, according to him, he controlled with two half-crowns. Did I think the M.O. would notice? Personally I did not give much for his chances. I said we could but hope for the best. The room allocated to the Medical Officer was the kitchen of the house occupied by RHQ. As was usual in houses built at that time it was small. We were paraded before the M.O. three at a time. 'Do you chaps feel all right?' he asked. We all said we did. 'O.K.' he said, 'A.1.' His orderly made necessary entries on our medical sheets and we marched out. Jimmy was ecstatic.

A day or two later we had to have our vaccination and

inoculations. One of the latter was known as 'TAB'. (I never did discover what this meant). That night I was on duty in the office. Three or four of us had to take turns spending the night there to sign for packets, which might be delivered by despatch riders. This was on top of our usual day. I had a fairly uneventful night and dozed most of the time. When the others arrived in the morning, however, I found that whenever I tried to speak I burst into tears. I could not get a word out. Curiously enough, apart from being rather tired I did not feel unwell. The others did not know what to do with me, but when the RSM came in he asked 'Did you have that bloody TAB jab yesterday'. I could not speak but nodded my head. 'That's what it was', he said, 'exactly the same thing happened to me when I had it for the first time, twenty years ago. Go back to your billet and get your head down for two or three hours.' I did so, had a deep sleep, and awoke that afternoon and found that I had fully recovered.

There was consternation one day in the regimental office. On mobilisation, all men under eighteen had to be posted to Woolwich Depot and a request had to be submitted for reservists to make up the numbers. In those days the number of car owners was comparatively few and was reflected in the number who could drive. Consequently the regiment badly needed drivers and asked for them accordingly. The reservists who appeared had all served in the Royal Artillery before it was mechanised and they were all horsemen. What our adjutant, a Territorial of course, did not know was that 'Drivers RA' still existed and that the drivers of vehicles were, in Army parlance, 'Drivers i/c'. The officer at the Reserve Depot who sent them to us was obviously either a fool or bloody-minded. Fortunately, several of them had become lorry drivers in civilian life.

Anne and I had long been committed to each other and, as the regiment was bound to be on the move shortly, the time seemed to be right for us to be formally engaged. During the second week of the war this feeling was reinforced when I discovered, somewhat dramatically, that not only were we to leave Cheam shortly, but what our destination would be.

One afternoon, we had cleared the boxes and crates which had arrived that day except for one which was well-made and quite heavy. It carried no markings of any sort and we had no document which related to it. The RQMS said we had better open it to see what it contained, so Jimmy and I got going with our jemmies. The top was well nailed down but we got it off eventually. The contents were covered with a sheet of paper. When we removed this we found the box contained 1:25,000 maps of Northern France. The RQMS went white. 'Put the top on again and take it to the regimental office', he said. 'And', he added, 'keep your mouths shut'.

The following Sunday, the 17th, I was given a leave pass for a whole nine hours, from 2 p.m. until 11 p.m. We were not told as much, but this was the only embarkation leave we were going to get. The pass included permission to travel to London. Anne and I told our families of our engagement and received their blessing.

The following day I heard that our transport, including the guns, of course, were to set off on the Thursday. Before then, however, we had a panic. Two days before they departed we received boxes of the webbing equipment which was then being introduced. This was extremely well designed to enable a soldier to carry everything necessary whilst still keeping arms free. Some items, such as packs, haversacks, water bottles and belts were easily identified but in addition there were straps of varying widths and lengths. No-one knew how to put it all together. Help had to be sought from a depot and urgent intensive training given to representatives of RHQ and the Batteries. It was as well that this course was adopted because everything depended, not only on the bits being put together properly, but also on the equipment being properly adjusted to each individual wearer. So the drivers were able to go off properly equipped.

We now knew we were all to depart shortly. Anne came to meet me on the Saturday and we bought her engagement ring. Mary had told Mrs Umney of our engagement and she invited Anne to our midday meal the following day. That evening, Mr Umney gave Jimmy and me some of his firm's products. He said that, judging from his experiences in the previous war, we would appreciate the disinfectant qualities of Wright's Coal Tar soap, together with some insect repellant ointment. He also gave us tubes of shaving cream which, he said, worked much better with cold water than the usual shaving stick. We found that he was right. We were grateful to him and his wife for the comfortable start they gave us to the war.

The next morning we marched to the railway station where we boarded a special train, which took us directly to Southampton docks.

3

25 September 1939

At Southampton we boarded a passenger ferry. (It was before the days of roll-on roll-off.) Members of a Medium Regiment of the RA had already boarded. We found some deck space on which to sit and enjoy the sunshine. We eventually moved down Southampton Water and caught up with another troopship. At Spithead we dropped anchor behind two more ships and lay there all the evening. Word went round that we were to sail at midnight and we set off about then. After only a short distance, however, we suddenly stopped. We heard later that the boom barring access to the open sea had been fouled by an enemy submarine which had been sunk. Eventually the obstacle was removed and we set off again in the small hours.

It was very dark. We could just see the ship ahead of us. Suddenly a destroyer passed us at what appeared to be great speed. It, or a companion, soon appeared on the other side going the other way. They were obviously circling the convoy to ward off German submarines. Our ship lurched at intervals as it changed course. Though the deck was not a comfortable bed, most of us managed to doze off. It was 8 a.m. when we arrived at Cherbourg. We disembarked and dumped our kit on the quay. Three and a half weeks after the regiment was mobilised and only four months since some of us had joined the Territorial Army as raw recruits we were on foreign soil as members of the British Expeditionary Force.

Six of us were ordered to guard the kit in pairs. Otherwise we could wander into the town, reporting back by 6 p.m. When I had finished my stint a gunner whom I did not know came up to me. 'Do you know French?', he asked. I said I did French at school but had left eight years ago, had never been in France before and had no idea how I would get on when I tried to speak it. 'That's all right', he said. 'Will you come and help me to buy a penknife?'. I agreed and as we walked into the town I racked my brains trying to remember the French for penknife. Was it 'canif'? We found a shop with a display of knives of all sizes and descriptions in the window. We were able to buy a suitable knife, but I felt we were able to do so more by gesticulating and pointing than by my use of the language. However, from then on I was marked as 'the one who could speak French'.

When we boarded a train we found it came up (or should I say down?) to our worst expectations. Our fathers had told us what French trains were like in their war. There had obviously been no improvement. The bare wooden seats were unspeakably uncomfortable and when we finally got moving the train dawdled and rattled along, with extra jolting as it passed over points. Eventually we managed to doze off. After all, the previous night had been spent on the equally hard deck of the ferry. I was woken by an application of the brakes and saw that it was daylight. I raised the blind and found that we were moving slowly through Le Mans station. We came to a halt in a siding. After a time there was a bump and we moved off in the opposite direction.

All the morning we rolled along through the Normandy countryside. Eventually we arrived at a small station labelled La Hutte and disembarked in a siding. After the usual wait (we were getting accustomed to waiting by this time) some RASC lorries arrived which took us to a charming village called Saint Rémy du Plain. It was not very big, but it had a Mairie. This was in an attractive four-square detached building over the door of which were flying the Tricolour and the Union Jack. I was told that I was now to help in the regimental office, which was set up in the small council chamber of the Mairie. As there was little going on as we awaited the arrival of our guns and vehicles, this meant that in practice I was to 'hold the fort' with Chalky White, another gunner clerk, whilst the officers and sergeant clerk took themselves off elsewhere for most of the time.

The following morning, Ernie Frayne, the assistant cook, came to the office and said that his sergeant wanted me to come at once to the cook-house. This was in a small building and yard not far from the Mairie. When I arrived I found that I was needed as a translator. My undeserved reputation had spread. A young woman, more smartly dressed than most women in the village, was trying to convey a message, but she could not speak a word of English. I managed to ascertain that she was the daughter of the man who owned the building and yard, a M. Blanchard, and that he was afraid the place would be burned down. The petrol-fired cooker certainly made a fearsome roar when it was in action and looked dangerous if used in a confined space. I was able to assure her that the building would be used only for food preparation and cooking would be carried out in the yard. I could only hope that the sergeant cook would keep to his word if it rained.

The following morning I was summoned to the cook-house again. The young lady had another complaint from her father, who apparently owned much of the village. This time it was quite a trivial matter and easily disposed of. She then gave me two eggs in gratitude for my help. These Chalky and I ate with relish with our tea of bread and margarine and jam.

One advantage of being in the office was that I overheard the colonel or adjutant when they telephoned Corps headquarters to ascertain when our transport would arrive. The only information they could get was that it had landed in France. It was four days before we heard that it had set off from Saint-Nazaire and should be in Saint Rémy that day. When the convoy was due we all crowded the pavement to watch it arrive. We were joined by local people, mostly women and children and older men, the young men having been called up.

Mlle Blanchard came and stood next to me and asked what was going on. I told her, hoping 'camion' and 'cannon' were the right words. I then found a young officer from one of the batteries standing on the other side of me. I did not know him but had seen him about the village and did not like his swash-buckling air. 'Does she do it?' he asked me quietly, nodding in Mlle Blanchard's direction. I was deliberately obtuse. 'Does she do what?' I asked. 'You know', he said nudging me in the ribs.

I was appalled. One had heard of the behaviour throughout the centuries of the 'rude licentious soldiery' of all nations. One did not expect, however, that an educated man who presumably regarded himself as a gentleman should, just because he was a soldier on foreign soil, think that any girl in the host country was fair game. I did not try to hide my contempt. 'If you think you have a chance, you'd better ask her', I said. As soon as I had spoken I realised the risk I was taking. If he did in fact proposition the girl, she would undoubtedly tell her father who would then complain to the maire and our colonel and there would be hell to pay. Fortunately, he walked away.

Whilst we were waiting for the convoy to arrive mademoiselle and I continued our conversation. She told me she had become engaged two weeks ago, before her fiancé, who was a Zouave, had left to join his regiment. She proudly displayed her engagement ring. I was able to tell her that I too had become engaged just before leaving England. The convoy then arrived. It was an imposing sight. There were about a hundred vehicles in all plus several motorcycles. Trucks ranged from 8 cwt to three-tonners. The 24 25-pounders, each towed behind its quad-ant and ammunition trailer, were both elegant and menacing. The LAD (Light Aid Detachment), then in the RAOC, with its large recovery vehicle, brought up the rear. The noise in the narrow street was deafening. The whole convoy passed us before being diverted to the gun and vehicle parks allocated to the various troops.

The drivers had had a wretched time since leaving Cheam over a week before. Waiting for loading to be completed at Avonmouth was no more than boring, but it was followed by four days at sea, and the Bay of Biscay had not been kind to some of them. Then, on arriving at Saint-Nazaire, they found there was a shortage of dockers so that they had to unload the guns and vehicles themselves. Finally, the long journey that day had been hot and dusty. They were not in a good mood, but a few beers and a good night's rest soon restored their spirits. Two or three days later, fully manned and equipped as a fighting unit, we set off towards what we all expected to be the battle-front.

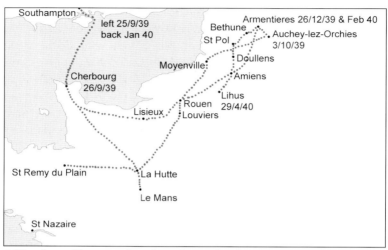

4 Northern France, showing the author's route.

It was my first experience of travelling in convoy. The rules for convoys are strict and the colonel insisted that they be complied with. For this journey, the vehicles were to travel 100 yards apart, as a precaution against air attacks. The speed was to be 30 mph. The success of the operation depended on the efficiency of the despatch riders (DRs) who 'shepherded' the convoy. Because there was civilian traffic on the road and we had to pass through towns and villages, interruptions occurred which meant that the vehicles in front had to be checked to prevent them from drawing away from those following, otherwise those behind would have to exceed the speed limit if they were to catch up. So far as transport was concerned, the colonel was not only insistent on convoy discipline, he was concerned with the maintenance of the vehicles themselves. Every Saturday morning, when we were not in action, he would don a boiler suit and visit one of the six troops and inspect every vehicle including the underside. Breakdowns through mechanical failure had to be avoided as far as possible. Any vehicle which did have to stop was dealt with by the mechanics of the LAD which brought up the rear. The importance of all this became obvious when we eventually went into action, when it was essential that the regiment should arrive complete wherever it was required.

Jimmy Bagley and I travelled in the back of Q2. This was an imprest truck, in other words a civilian vehicle taken into military service. It was, in fact, a Guy furniture pantechnicon with good suspension and a smooth-running engine. It carried a load of blankets and Jimmy and I made ourselves comfortable among them. The weather was beautiful and cruising through the Normandy countryside very pleasant. It reminded me of South Devon.

It became quite hot in the sunshine so, when having halted for a short break we found ourselves opposite a prosperous-looking farmhouse, I decided to try to buy some of the cider for which that part of the country is famous. The farmer was reluctant but eventually agreed to sell me a litre. In the heat of the afternoon the drink was most acceptable and we emptied the bottle between us. The next we knew we were being woken up in Louviers, that day's destination. I learned that this cider, like home-brewed West Country scrumpy, has a high alcohol content and the locals usually drank it diluted with water. Regimental HQ was again lodged in the town's mairie, so again we slept on a municipal floor. Two of the reservists, who spoke no French but, like old soldiers everywhere, were of great resource, had arranged for a local family to provide a roast chicken dinner for six at a modest price. They invited Jimmy and me to join them and we accepted with enthusiasm.

The next day we went through Rouen. We had a sight of the magnificent cathedral, but my abiding memory of the city is of our first encounter with the French army. Poilus were on duty at street crossings and outside public buildings. They looked too old for combat service. They were clad in shabby old blue uniforms and most of them had their tin helmets tilted to the back of the head. They wore several days growth of beard. They either leaned against a convenient wall, their rifles hanging from their shoulders, or used their rifles as props. Most of them had a cigarette drooping from a corner of the mouth. It was not a pretty sight.

We stopped that night in Moyenville, a village not far from Abbeville. Our accommodation here was a dance hall. When Jimmy and I arrived it was crowded and nearly all the wall space was occupied. Worse, the floor had been liberally sprinkled with French chalk, particles of which could be seen floating in the air. I elected to sleep on a ledge barely two feet wide. It was precarious and uncomfortable, but better than filling my lungs with French chalk.

On a shed door nearby was chalked 'C Coy HQ' and there were similar 'mementoes' of the First World War throughout the village. I doubt whether, after twenty odd years they could genuinely have been the original markings, but they, and the towns we passed through the next day, including Arras and Douai, reminded us that we were now in the area where our fathers had fought.

4

3 October 1939

So, after travelling over four hundred miles in three days without losing a vehicle through accident or breakdown, we arrived in Auchy-lez-Orchies. This was a small village a few miles from the Belgian frontier, about a mile from the market town of Orchies. RHQ was installed in a building fronting the road. Behind this was a small yard and beyond that the courtyard of the largest house in the village. This was approached through an arch through the front building, leaving a small room on one side. The ground floor of the main part of the building was occupied by the colonel's and the general offices and the Royal Signals' exchange. A room at the back was used as a cookhouse. In the yard was a pump, which was the only source of water.

All the Other Ranks slept in a large room on the floor above. We were issued with palliasse and straw with which to fill them. Apart from this comparative comfort, the accommodation was bleak, with a complete lack of privacy. I looked around, however, and found a small room above the arch, which was normally used as an apple loft. This was just big enough for three of us. There was not much headroom, but it was cosy.

I was told that I was still needed as a clerk. I shared a small room on the other side of the arch with Sgt Noton. He spoke French fluently and did most of the liaison work with the locals. My basic responsibility was for the paperwork relating to RHQ personnel, mostly the preparation of the acquittance rolls which men had to sign when receiving their pay. This, however, did not take much time and I worked mostly in the general office. My first job there was to deal with some of the forms with which I had wrestled at Beaulieu camp. The RA Records office had kindly sent them to us in France to dot a few 'i's and cross a few 't's. I was then confronted with a mammoth task. The office had been issued with two large books—King's Regulations and the Manual of Military Law—together with a large file of Army Council Instructions. Each of these was accompanied by several booklets of amendments, which had been published over several years. Often there were amendments of amendments. They were printed on one side of the paper only and the favoured method of entering them was to cut each one out and paste it over the relevant part of the original. As they often consisted of only a line or two, this was a fiddly job. Each amendment then had to be numbered and dated. To make sure each one was in the appropriate place it was necessary to read the context. The knowledge which in so doing I gained of these books and documents which ruled Army life stood me in good stead when I later became a Sergeant Artillery Clerk.

One advantage of working in RHQ was that one got a fair idea of what was going on. This was denied to most soldiers, whose knowledge was virtually restricted to the activities of their own units. I found that we were one of four Territorial artillery regiments—the 91st, 92nd, 97th and 98th Army Field Regiments —under the command of 1 Corps (hence the 'Army' in our title). All of these regiments had distinguished themselves in recent years in gunnery competitions. Corps HQ was in Douai, but the Corps Commander, Royal Artillery (CCRA) had his HQ in a secluded house a mile or so up the road from us. He set about bringing the Territorial units up to the standard of the Regulars. Each unit, soon after we arrived, set about digging gun pits and slit trenches in its allotted sector near the Belgian frontier, but this work was interrupted by a busy round of exercises, gunnery practice on a firing range and officers' TEWTS (tactical exercises without troops).

A day or two after we arrived in Auchy, the colonel sent for me. He asked me about my civilian background and then said he was going to appoint me regimental postal orderly. He gave me a chit (Army-speak for a small piece of paper) authorising me to collect mail from the Army Post Office at Corps HQ and to sign for any registered mail. This meant going to Douai every morning. Transport would be provided by each Battery and RHQ in turn and, because it was the colonel's policy for every man to be able to drive, I was to do all the driving under the supervision of the vehicle's own driver. This posed no difficulty so far as RHQ was concerned as the vehicle allocated was Q2, the former furniture van, which was easy to drive and whose driver, Murray, was both friendly and helpful. It was not so popular with the Battery drivers who hated their beloved vehicles to be subjected to the possible abuse of a learner. Making the return journey to Douai and distributing the mail took up most of my mornings. It made a change from routine work in the office.

One afternoon, after I had been doing my new job for about a week, Captain King walked into my office. He was an RHQ officer, but my duties had not previously brought me into contact with him. 'My driver is sick, so you can drive me, Wild', he said. 'I have some visits to make'. I protested that I had only just begun to learn to drive, but he insisted that he wanted to see how I was getting on. We went outside to his 8 cwt truck, a type which I pointed out I had never driven. 'It's the same as a 15 cwt', he said. Our first call was in Orchies, at a building in the market square. When we got there the market was in full swing. The square was packed with stalls and people, who spilled out across the narrow perimeter road. The captain alighted at the building where he was calling. 'You can't park here: drive round the square until I come out', he ordered. So I drove slowly round and round the square, thankfully missing the pedestrians wandering about, chatting in groups. Suddenly, he jumped out immediately in front of me. I slammed my feet down on brake and clutch and stopped about a foot away from him. Unfortunately, however, my clumsy Army boot caught the side of the accelerator pedal, causing the powerful engine to give a mighty roar. King was furious, declaring I had done it on purpose to scare him. It certainly scared me!

We drove on in silence until, going through a small town, my passenger suddenly shouted 'Stop'. I slammed on the brakes and he hit his head on the windscreen, knocking his hat askew. 'Why did you do that?' he demanded. I said that, from the way he shouted I thought it was an emergency. It was not, of course. He had suddenly caught sight of the entrance to the officers' mess, which was his next port of call. He told me to go to the kitchen to get a cup of tea. I spent a pleasant hour drinking tea with one of the mess orderlies, discussing the demerits of our respective officers and other topics dear to the hearts of squaddies, until King put his head round the door and said 'I'm going to ride with my friend. Follow us'.

I grabbed my cap and hurried out, buttoning up the neck of my blouse as I went. I got out just in time to see the other officer's truck moving off. By the time I got started he had got well away and I had to put my foot down if I was to catch up, driving faster than ever before. Not long after, the tail-light of the other vehicle came on and I realised it was getting dark. I had no idea where to find the switches controlling the lights. I fiddled with everything I could feel on the dashboard until, to my relief, I found the right one. Meantime, the other truck had got well ahead and I had to speed up again. This was hazardous in the dark, as we only had side-lights, and even these were partially obscured. After what seemed ages, I caught up with the other vehicle and soon afterwards it stopped and King joined me. Except for when he gave me directions, we did not speak. I felt like telling him what I thought of the way he had treated me, but knew that if I did so he would probably charge me with insubordination. We reached Auchy safely. He never ordered me to drive him again. I wondered how he would have fared if I had finished up in a ditch and a Court of Inquiry had been convened.

We were warned in daily orders that there were spies about, whose mission was to discover the number and location of British units. We had obtained some typing stencils from Corps RAHQ and I walked one day to their office to run them off on their Gestetner. The distance was about a mile along a straight road with nothing to see but flat fields of sugar beet on either side. I had nearly reached the turning leading to the HQ when I met a huge fellow in the sort of rough clothing worn by farm workers. He stopped me and asked if I could tell him where to find the Hampshire Regiment. He explained that they had had some photographs taken but had been moved before they were ready and he wanted to deliver them and collect his money. He did not look like a photographer. He produced some sepia prints of a group of soldiers dressed in the service dress of the previous war, with flat caps and long puttees. He was an obvious phoney, but I was in a quandary. There was no-one in sight in either direction. I was unarmed and would certainly lose if it came to a fight. To take him to Corps RAHQ was out of the question, but our RHQ in the village was on the village road and there for all to see. I told the man I did not know where the Hampshires were, but that if he went to our office in the village I was sure they would be able to help him. He thanked me and I walked quickly to my destination. As soon as I reached there I telephoned my office and told them what had happened so that they could get the man apprehended when he arrived. I ran off the copies we needed on the Gestetner and returned to my HQ. I asked if the man had turned up. 'No', said my sergeant in his usual bored tones. 'We haven't seen him'. I was piqued that no-one had gone out into the lane to intercept an obvious spy.

I received a letter from the minister of the church which I attended. He had for a long time been a confirmed pacifist and I respected him and his views. He had supported men who had to appear before conscientious objectors' tribunals. He wrote to say how glad he was to hear that I was a clerk and would not have to fire guns to kill people. I replied that the gun teams could not operate without the support of the surveyors, drivers, cooks, clerks and orderlies who made up the majority of the unit. All of us shared the responsibility of the man on the gun, as did the rest of the army, including the RAMC, in which some of his protégés had elected to serve, and indeed all who did not oppose the war effort. I had given much thought in the past as to what action I should take in the event of war, in view of my Christian beliefs. I decided that if it happened I could not stand aside, which is why I enlisted in the Territorial Army.

We soon found that there was little to do in Auchy after duty each day. Some played endless games of cards in the sleeping quarters. A few could apparently afford to drink in the only estaminet all the evening. A pass was required to leave the immediate area, but this was of no significance because there was no public transport anyway. I was fortunate in that my postal duties at least gave me a daily change of scene. I was lucky in the draw to see a show in Lille in which George Formby was the star performer. Otherwise, the only way to get out of the village for recreational purposes was to take our turn to be taken by truck (popularly known as the 'passion wagon') to Douai for a few hours on a Saturday afternoon. There was little to do, however, when one got there.

My two companions and I spent most evenings lying on our palliasse in the apple loft. We ate sweet biscuits (there were usually packets in the parcels we got from home) and soft cheeses which I bought in Orchies market on the way to Douai. Peter Gascoigne and Bob Paxton both worked in the Croydon Corporation electricity department. Peter was the colonel's driver and was very proud of the Humber for which he was responsible. Bob was designated the RSM's batman and did all sorts of menial duties. The unit was short of clerks and I tried to get him to apply to be one. 'I do clerking for a living', he said. 'I'm not going to do it on my holidays'. He maintained this attitude throughout the war. It was not long before we ran out of topics of conversation, even allowing for Peter's fund of (mostly blue) stories.

Our unit had the use of the parish hall and Noton, having somehow got permission to visit Paris, was able to hire a cinematograph projector and some American films, mostly musicals. They were, however, dubbed in French except for the songs, and so were unintelligible to us. Noton was unable to get hold of the films in their original form, or even of French films with English sub-titles.

We heard that the family at a house round the corner, a small holding where eggs were for sale, might supply eggs and chips, at that time the favourite evening snack of the British soldier. We went to see if this was so and found that the house had a large room formerly used for community purposes. This we could hire at a modest rent and egg and chips could be provided. We decided to form a club. About twenty men in RHQ were

5 Membership card for RHQ club.

interested. I typed a 'membership card' for which each man gave a franc a week to pay the rent. The room already had folding card tables and chairs and we obtained through the padre chess and draughts boards and sets, darts, games like Ludo and packs of playing cards.

Here I must refer to Taffy. He was one of the three despatch riders in RHQ. He was a son of the South Wales Valleys. His every utterance was not merely spoken: it was declaimed in a loud voice in his rich Welsh accent. He was immensely proud of the Royal Artillery and told of vast parades in India where the Gunners took precedence—'Right of the Line and Pride of the British Army', he declared. He was also proud to be a 'DonR'. He was, however, a rogue. Led by him, the DRs seemed to roam at will on their machines and so far as I know they were never caught out. He boasted of stealing from shops and market stalls. He told with glee of the halcyon days before the war, when he was training at Shorncliffe, how he and his cronies would spend evenings beating up and robbing homosexuals (he did not call them that) who frequented the Leas at Folkestone. According to him, women yielded to his charms readily and he would persist in recounting in graphic detail the seduction and sexual perform-ance of each. I did not consider him a nice person.

He came into the club one day when some of us were playing Pontoon and we invited him to join us. 'No', he said 'It wouldn't be fair'. He went on to tell us how, after leaving the pit after the last shift of the week, men would gamble and drink away all the wages they had collected before going home. We, he said, did not know what real gambling was nor what we would be up against if he joined us. 'I'll show you', he said, and sat down. After two or three hands the bank came to him. We never shuffled the pack, but simply gathered up the cards as they lay on the table. He took the pack and, when it had been cut, took each card from the top in succession and before turning it over said what its value would be. He was hardly ever wrong. 'Playing with you lot I'd clean you all out', he said, and left. There was a good side to Taffy after all.

5

October 1939

It was understandable that in sending troops into what was expected to be a battle zone at any time, the Army did not concern itself with what the men could do with themselves when off duty. It was a remarkable effort to get so many combat troops into France so speedily. The same effort was apparently not given to backing them up with support services. For instance, although all were entitled to a tobacco ration, no cigarettes came to the troops for week after week. As Virginia cigarettes were not stocked by French shops, this was a source of grievance to the majority of men, who were cigarette smokers. As a pipe smoker, I was happy to receive my ounce of Gold Block every week. (Pull up the ladder, Jack!)

After about a month a mobile laundry and bath unit arrived a few miles away, so that, with luck, we were able to get a hot shower and a change of underwear every week or so. It was evident that hygiene did not come high in the list of priorities of the British Army in the field.

As Territorials and Reservists we each had only one uniform and one pair of boots. After a week or two in Auchy it began to rain, and it rained incessantly. All the gun positions were flooded and drainage methods had to be devised (not an easy task in that terrain). Our boots were badly in need of repair but the quartermaster could do nothing about it because he had no clothing spares at all. Fed up with permanently wet feet, I bought myself a pair of ankle length rubber boots and actually got permission to wear them on parade! At last supplies of boots arrived and we were issued, not with one pair but with two! With them came a Command order that in future boots must be dubbined and no boot polish was to be used.

I was in the office when the Second-in-Command told the

RSM to instruct the men accordingly. 'Ah', said the RSM, 'that means the boots they use for work must be dubbined and the other pair kept properly polished'. 'It means, sergeant major,' said the 2 i/c, 'that both pairs will be dubbined'. At the parade the next morning the RSM said 'From now on all boots will be dubbined, but in RHQ they'll *look* as though they've been properly polished'. He knew perfectly well, of course, that it was impossible to keep the boots black without the use of polish, because if only dubbin were used they would soon become grey.

Soon after this we were issued with a second uniform and a greatcoat. A few days later we heard that the King was to visit the troops. There may have been no connection between the two events, but the modem British soldier is a born cynic. On the appointed day we paraded outside our HQ—much too early, of course. Eventually the cars we were awaiting came into view. We were called to attention, the officer saluted, and the cars swept by, hardly slackening speed. We caught a glimpse of staff officers, one of whom was the King, and that was it. Still, we appreciated the King coming to see us and if it prompted those responsible to do something about sending us our new uniforms, he was more than welcome.

When the rain stopped at last, it started getting colder. Soon the pump in the yard froze every night and we had to hang about in the morning until the cooks had got it working with the aid of boiling water. Washing and shaving in the very cold water was a miserable experience and I blessed Mr Umney for his shaving cream which was as effective in these conditions as he had claimed it would be.

If I have conveyed the impression that conditions for us in Auchy were harsh, I can only confess that that was my intention. For the officers it was entirely different. Whilst the troops slept on the floor on palliasse in one large room, they were billeted in private houses, had rooms to themselves and slept in comfortable beds. Instead of waiting in the yard for the pump to be unfrozen so that they could get water in which to wash and shave, they had the use of bathrooms, with all the hot water they required. Well off as most of them were, I doubt whether any of them had enjoyed the ministrations of a manservant in civilian life, but here each of them had a batman. The officers of each battery argued about the relative comfort of their messes which, they claimed, were veritable homes from homes. The daily diet of the men was dull in the extreme. The main meal invariably consisted of stewed beef followed by 'Chinese wedding cake' (rice boiled with some sultanas). The officers were able to supplement their rations with extra food from the shops, including French delicacies. They had their own cooks in each mess who were able, the officers claimed, to produce meals of a gourmet standard. Whilst the men were confined to the village, there appeared to be no restrictions on the use by officers of military transport for recreational purposes and there was much discussion as to the merits of restaurants in Douai and Lille. The Café Metropole in the latter was such a favourite with both French and British that it was an unofficial international officers' club. For most of the officers this was, so far, a lovely war.

Curiously enough, I never heard any criticism of this difference between the conditions enjoyed by the officers and those endured by the Other Ranks. It was regarded as the natural order of things, to be accepted without question. The same attitude persisted when I myself was commissioned later in the war, though being on home soil the men were then housed mostly in permanent or temporary barracks and slept on bedsteads or two-tier bunks. (Those in camps were not so lucky.) Also, the Army Catering Corps had come into being, ensuring that unit cooks were properly trained and supervised. The same unquestioning attitude was unaltered during my years of service in various Army reserves and so far as I know it is still the same today.

An order was received from the War Office that Sgt Noton and a gunner in one of the batteries were to be sent home on leave for fourteen days, during which time they were to be kitted out as officers and return to the regiment as second lieutenants. They had applied for Territorial Army commissions some months before and meanwhile had enlisted in the ranks. Their applications had now been approved. Noton was obviously suitable to be an officer. The other man, however, had been switched from job to job and was described by his Battery Sergeant-Major as a 'useless twit'. Territorial Army officers were apparently expected to receive all their training in their units. This worked in peace time, as was proved when the TA was called upon to fight, but to send two men, with no training whatsoever, to serve in a regiment which might be in action at any time seemed ludicrous. On his return from leave, Noton carried on doing the job he had done as a sergeant. What the battery did with the other man I cannot guess.

Meanwhile, the CO had selected some sergeants whom he considered to be potential officers. They were all experienced No. 1's (a Number One is the sergeant in charge of a gun). They had been promoted to the temporary rank of Warrant Officer Class 3 and called Troop Sergeant-Majors. They had to go through the usual procedure for emergency commissions, which involved appearance before a War Office Selection Board (WOSB) before being posted to an Officer Cadet Training Unit (OCTU).

A Command Order then instructed CO's to recommend suitable men for officer training. It stipulated, however, that candidates must be corporals or above. On the face of it this was reasonable, but it was not so in every case. For example, most of the signalmen in the Royal Corps of Signals attached to us were old boys of either Bedford School or Bedford Modern School. They joined up en masse when the TA was brought up to strength, into a unit which already had its complement of NCOs. None of them was eligible for consideration, nor likely to be in the near future.

At home, an office colleague of mine was called up with his age group soon after the outbreak of war. He did his initial training at Woolwich Depot, immediately after which he was sent on a Junior Leaders' course. At the end of this he appeared before a WOSB, proceeded to an OCTU and was commissioned in the summer of 1940. He was a man unquestionably suitable for commissioned rank, but why he should have had preference over volunteers of similar education and background I cannot understand.

I mention these occurrences, not because they affected me in any way, but because they illustrate the peculiar attitude of the War Office to the granting of commissions at that time.

6

11 November 1939

On Armistice Day we paraded for a service in the parish churchyard, in front of the graves of four British soldiers. They were all killed in the final advance of the Allies in 1918, a short time before the Armistice was declared. All four were under twenty years of age. Nothing could have demonstrated more forcefully the wastefulness and futility of war. Yet here we were, only twenty-one years later, fighting the same enemy over the same territory.

Submission to the domination of the Nazis was out of the question, so our country had no choice but to fight and it was up to us and the rest of the armed forces to try to finish the job which our fathers' generation thought that they themselves had completed at a terrible cost. It was an unforgettable emotional experience, one which has so far as I am concerned been repeated every year since on Remembrance Day.

The adjutant became seriously ill and had to be sent home. His replacement was a Regular captain. He was a serious young man who strode rather than walked about. This and the fact that his lower jaw was naturally thrust forward gave him a stern, almost menacing appearance which was at odds with what I later discovered to be his true personality. He was a professional soldier through and through and my impression when he came was that he thought he had a mission to 'lick these amateurs into shape'. He soon settled in, probably finding that the job was not so difficult as he had feared.

The daily morning parade of RHQ personnel was normally conducted by the RSM, when he passed on any orders and allocated jobs as necessary. Occasionally, the parade was called by the Second-in-Command, who was responsible for our administration. For these parades the preliminaries were conducted by Captain King who then handed over to the 2 i/c. One morning, when such a parade was called, the captain did not appear and the preliminaries were conducted by the RSM. 'Where is Captain King?' the 2 i/c demanded as he returned the RSM's salute. 'He is not on parade, Sir', was the reply— something which was pretty obvious. 'Wild', said the 2 i/c, 'Do you know where Captain King is billeted?'. I said I did. 'Fall out and go and remind him that parade was ordered for 0900 hours'. I did as I was told and found my way to King's bedroom. He was fast asleep. I shook his shoulder and said 'I've been sent to remind you that parade was at 0900'. 'Piss off', was his elegant reply. 'OK', I said as I left the room, 'but it was the 2 i/c who sent me and he is bloody furious'. He leapt out of bed, swearing violently, and appeared on the parade ground just as we were being dismissed. I would love to have been a fly on the wall when the 2 i/c interviewed him. He was far from being one of my favourite officers and it does me no credit to confess that I got malicious pleasure from his well-deserved discomfiture.

Chalky's 21st birthday occurred early in December. It was on a Saturday, but he was on duty that afternoon. After our midday meal we went over to the estaminet and I bought him an 'Oxford'. This was a beer produced especially for British soldiers by a local brewer—Mott-Cordinier—and was quite good. As I raised my glass to him in salute some of our friends there asked what we were celebrating. We told them and there was an immediate chorus of 'Have one with me'. A whole row of drinks lined up in front of Chalky. I had one or two beers myself but realised that if Chalky drank all that had been given him—they were mostly liqueurs—he would be in no condition to work. I reminded him that he was due back in the office, but he replied 'Tha's all righ'. I'll go in a minute'. As he obviously had no intention of doing so, I went over to take his place. I was not officially a RHQ clerk, but knew enough to fill in if necessary.

There was nobody in the office when I arrived. I was not used to drinking beer in the middle of the day and settled down for a doze. I was disturbed by the arrival of the Maréchal de Logis, the official name for our French Liaison Officer. He cut a magnifi-

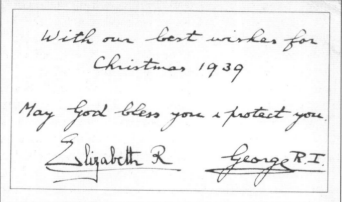

With our best wishes for
Christmas 1939

May God bless you & protect you.

Elizabeth R   George R.I.

6 The Royal Christmas card to the Armed Forces, 1939.

cent figure. He was tall and distinguished, clad in a very smart service dress with two rows of medal ribbons, including the Croix de Guerre. He had a grand air and was extremely voluble. I had often heard him holding forth to our officers of his experiences in Paris. He apparently operated on the fringes of the political establishment and had many scandalous tales to tell of intrigue and even corruption in that milieu.

'Can you type in French?', he demanded. I said I would try. He gave me a letter he had drafted, for signature by the colonel, to the parish priest, inviting the children of the village to a party, which our officers proposed to hold for them. Halfway through the task I stopped. 'That's wrong', I said and pointed out what I thought was a grammatical error. He snatched up the draft. 'Mon Dieu', he exclaimed, 'You're right. Thank you'. Afterwards I realised what cheek I had shown in criticising a Frenchman's French. I can only ascribe my boldness to the influence of alcohol.

Christmas was memorable. We all had cards and parcels from home, of course, and a card from the King and Queen, which I still have. On Christmas morning we were woken by the sergeants bringing us tea laced with rum. We had a leisurely late breakfast, then there was a church parade. After the short service, the colonel to our surprise led us for a march up the road for a mile. We turned round and marched back. Outside RHQ, the colonel said 'I've taken you for a walk so that no-one has the chance to spoil his dinner by drinking too much beforehand. Now go and enjoy your dinner. A merry Christmas'.

Dinner was magnificent—pork, a meat for special occasions in those days, baked potatoes, sprouts etc., followed by Christmas pudding. The RASC and the cooks had achieved a standard which we had reason to believe was beyond them. Various well-wishers had provided beer, sweets and cigarettes, which had been in short supply. Given that we could not be among our loved ones, it was a happy day. The next morning, however, we were brought down to earth with a bump.

We paraded at our normal time, several of the men with a hang-over. They came to life with a jerk when the RSM announced 'We are moving today. Everything is to be packed ready to move by 1700 hours'. He gave us instructions where to empty our palliasse of straw and dished out the jobs which were to be done.

We moved off at 1800 hours. It was, of course, pitch dark. Soon after we started, it began to snow—large flakes, which settled lazily on everything. They rapidly increased in intensity and we arrived four hours later at our destination, which was Armentières, in a snow storm.

7

26 December 1939

In Armentières RHQ occupied 80 Route Nationale, which was normally the home of a family which, it was evident, was very rich. It was said the bathrooms had gold plated taps, but I never had the chance to see if this was so. The ground floor was used as offices, the first floor for officers' accommodation and the junior ranks slept in two large rooms on the top floor. We again slept on straw-filled palliasse, but at least it was warm, for the house was centrally heated.

As we were nearly all Londoners, we found the briskness and bustle of the town much more to our taste than the dull boredom of Auchy. Armentières seemed prosperous, with smart shops and many cafés (our equivalent of pubs). The town clock played a tune on its carillon every quarter of an hour—I think it was a phrase from *L'Arlesienne*. We were especially pleased when an order was received for us not to carry our gas masks. This made sense because the civilian population had not been issued with any. We shared the town with the 1st Green Howards, but there was never any trouble between the troops, even in their cups. They kept to the southern area and we to the northern. In between was situated the 'Black Cat', a brothel, which was out of bounds to both units.

We found that our move was to join the 5th Division, which meant that we dropped the 'Army' from our title. The 5th was a proud Regular front-line division which had, however, only one field regiment of artillery—the 9th. We and the 91st Field Regiment were drafted in to bring it up to strength. The Commander, Royal Artillery (CRA) set about bringing the two Territorial regiments up to the standard of the 9th, who considered themselves the best, so an intensive bout of further training began almost immediately.

After a few days, Chalky heard that two elderly sisters who had a hat shop in the Place de la République, just round the corner from RHQ, had a room which they had previously let to two members of the unit which were billeted in the place before us. They would also provide an evening meal. We found that we could get permission to sleep out so, though we could only just afford it, we decided to take the room.

The office was running very short of stationery and the sergeant had been unable to get supplies from official sources. On the afternoon of the day we were to move in to our lodgings, he gave me a shopping list and some money and told me to buy what I could. The list included typing paper, carbons, pencils (this was before the days of biros), paper clips and even a typewriter ribbon. I set off and was surprised to find a very smart office supplies shop. Inside, a dignified, superior-looking young lady gave the impression of presiding over formalities rather than being engaged in the sordid business of selling. She spoke no English, but I was able to convey to her what I needed. She was able to supply everything. She made out an invoice, I paid her and she gave me a receipt. She then made my purchases into a neat parcel. I picked it up and was about to leave when she raised a hand. 'Un moment', she said. I saw that she had taken another sheet of paper and was doing some calculations. When she had finished she put a few francs and some coins of small denomination on the counter and turned the paper towards me indicating that she wanted me to sign it. I must have looked puzzled for she took a French-English and English-French dictionary from the stock on the shelves and after searching through it said 'Commission. Pour vous. C'est convenable'. If it was 'convenable' I assumed it must be all right, so I picked up the money and thanked her.

On the way back to the office I passed a patisserie the window of which was full of 'gâteaux des rois' of various sizes. I realised that the next day was Epiphany. I spent the money I had just acquired on a cake big enough for four. We took it with us when we went to our lodging that evening and presented it to our landladies. They were delighted and declared that tomorrow we would celebrate the 'Fête des Rois'. They duly provided the next evening a meal of six delicious courses at the end of which we cut the cake. In its box there was a paper crown and in the cake a little china crown. The one who found this token in his portion of cake was solemnly crowned king of the evening.

They told us that some friends of theirs had invited them and us to dinner the following week. We accepted and went with them when the day came. The friends were a bank clerk and his wife. We were greeted with a glass of port as an aperitif. We then sat at the table. Before each course (and there must have been at least nine of them) our host, who was a small man with a prematurely receding hair line, dived into his cellar, the door to which opened into the kitchen in which we were seated. He emerged with a bottle and gave a speech about where the wine came from and its properties. After two or three courses, the alcohol began to take effect, he became more pompous and speeches longer and more rambling. At the same time the conversation generally became more lively. This was hard on me because none of the French spoke English and Chalky had no French. Accordingly, I was expected to try to translate everything everybody said. Chalky and I were subject to a 2200 hours curfew and I suddenly noticed we had passed that time. It would have been churlish, however, to have left in the middle of the proceedings.

We were drinking coffee after the last course when our host hauled himself to his feet once more. 'Now', he said, 'the Napoléon'. 'Not the Napoléon', begged his wife. The Napoléon was apparently a particularly fine brandy kept for very special occasions. 'The Napoléon', insisted the little man and dived once more through the cellar door. We toasted each other and our respective nations, congratulated Madame on her exquisite cooking and finally got on our way. It was now well past 11 p.m. but luckily we did not come across any redcaps in the few streets we had to traverse and we reached our lodgings safely. It had been an evening to remember.

Snow continued to fall for several days after we arrived in Armentières. It compacted into solid ice on the roads and was at least a foot deep. All military traffic was banned unless it was essential. The ban did not apply to my postal duties. In the bitter cold, one of the drivers and I found an isolated estaminet on the way where we could park our truck at the back and warm ourselves with a coffee and brandy.

Murray and I were sent to a depot in the suburbs of Lille to collect fresh supplies of heating oil for the house. We took two empty drums—huge things which, standing on end occupied almost the entire floor space of Q2. We found the depot without difficulty and full drums were loaded in place of the empty ones. They were so heavy that the vehicle went well down on its springs. Whilst I went into the office to sign a receipt, Murray drove Q2 to the front of the building. When I emerged I found him sitting in the passenger seat. In spite of my protestations he insisted that I should drive. 'It's no good you learning to drive if you never have experience of slippery conditions', he said. I drove off gingerly and on the smooth hard surface, with no difficult bends to negotiate and no other traffic, found it fairly easy. As we approached an intersection, I touched the brake to slow down. The truck sailed on, seeming to gather speed as it went. We skidded right across the other road, but fortunately nothing was coming the other way. 'That'll teach you', said Murray happily. 'How many times have I told you to keep your foot off the bloody brake pedal?'. It was an article of faith with Army drivers always to drive on the engine, using the brakes only in an emergency. I had learned my lesson.

Chalky and I got places on a passion wagon to Lille. We were set down in a shabby residential area and did not know in which direction we should go. Two of the older men, however, said 'Let's find a beer' and set off. This seemed as good an idea as any so we followed them along some nondescript and unlikely looking streets. We came to a building, which looked like a comer shop except that its windows were obscured. 'This'll do', one of the leaders said. Sure enough, inside there was a bar. We sat round a large table and a girl came to get our orders. At the back of the room was a group of women engaged in a heated discussion. It was dominated by a tall girl wearing a smart grey jacket and skirt. She had the appearance and bearing of a superior secretary. They spoke too quickly for me to gather what they were talking about, but I picked up a few words. Our beer arrived and most of the women marched towards the door. They stopped for their ringleader to harangue an old woman, dressed in black bombazine, seated at a small table. She said nothing but simply shrugged her shoulders. I then realised what it was all about. The women were refusing to work on a Saturday afternoon. They marched out.

One of the remaining women came and sat at our table. I thought she looked repulsive. She wore eye black and lipstick but her face was shiny all over as though covered with some sort of grease. 'Vich of you boys iss going to slip wiz me?' she demanded. I then realised how naive most of us had been. The men who had led us here said they wanted to do so. They had obviously been here before. The rest of us finished our drinks and left except for one young soldier who shocked us by saying he was going to stay. Though we urged him not to he refused to come with us. Thus easily are some apparently well brought up youngsters led astray when away from their families.

8

January 1940

The adjutant sent for me. 'We have to send one officer and one NCO to Larkhill for a Counter Battery course', he said. 'I know you wanted to be a surveyor, but I think this would suit you just as well'. He explained that the purpose of Counter Battery work was to locate enemy artillery so that it could be engaged and if possible neutralised. This was a primary task for medium artillery, which came under Corps command, so that it was possible that after the course I would be posted to a Corps HQ. I pointed out that I was not an NCO. 'That's easy', he said. So I became an unpaid acting lance-bombardier. A few days later a truck took me to Amiens station. On the platform I met a bombardier from another regiment and found we were going on the same course. We got a compartment to ourselves but it was not comfortable lying on the hard seats. The carriages were not heated although the train was to go right across France to Saint-Nazaire. It got unbearably cold. I remembered that in my haversack I had a quarter-bottle of brandy intended as a present for my father. I am afraid we drank the lot between us and my father was unlucky.

We arrived at Lisieux, where we had to change, soon after daybreak, which was not very early at that time of the year. We had intended to go into the town in search of coffee. We found that the station is at the bottom of a steep hill, on top of which stands the massive monastery, which dominates the town. There were some small shops opposite the station so we went to investigate them. The only sign of life we found was a barber who was just opening up. We thought a shave would be a good idea. It was the first time I had been shaved with a cut-throat razor and I did not enjoy the experience, especially as the barber was far from friendly. When he had finished we looked in the

mirror and saw that round where we had been shaved there was
a tide mark. We asked the barber if we could wash, but all he
would do was give us some wet-wipes with which we did our
best to clean off the grime.

In Cherbourg we had to report to the transit camp. This was
a dreary place, an old barracks, which had been vacated by the
French army. We were each issued with two blankets, which
smelt and felt filthy. The room where we were told to sleep had
a fireplace from which the cinders and ash of a long-dead coal
fire had not been cleared. After an early breakfast, we handed in
our blankets and were issued with haversack rations. Most of the
troops bound for the UK were a noisy, rowdy lot of Scottish
youngsters who were being sent back because they were under-
age. The morning was very misty. We were marched to the quay
where we boarded the ferry. The mist persisted and the ship did
not move. We ate our haversack rations and finally, in the early
evening, we were told to disembark. We were marched back to
the transit camp for a repeat of the previous night. The following
morning it was still as misty but to our surprise the ship moved
off soon after we had boarded.

The ship was so slow that it rolled in the calm sea as if it was
stationary. We pottered on all day until the early evening when
we stopped off the Isle of Wight. Here the news went round that
we could proceed no further until the morning because the boom
across Southampton Water was in place. The young Scotsmen,
who like the rest of us were hungry and frustrated, threatened to
become riotous. 'Come on', one of a group of them shouted as
they ran past us. 'We are going to rush the bridge'. We hastily
withdrew in the opposite direction. There was nothing we could
do to stop them. We were relieved when, before what could have
been a nasty incident occurred, it was announced over the ship's
Tannoy that the boom was being removed so that we could
proceed.

We had met up with four more bombardiers who were going
on the Counter Battery course and when we docked in Southampton we went, as were our instructions, to the Rail Transport
Officer's office. Here we found the six officers who were also on

the course. (Mine, I was not pleased to find, was the one with whom I had had the brush at Saint Rémy.) They took no notice of us. They were clustered around the RTO's table and had borrowed his telephone, on which one of them was speaking to Larkhill. When he had finished he told the others 'We need not report until the first lecture on Monday'. Without a word to any of us they then left. We put our heads together and agreed that we would each declare that 'one of the officers', unknown to us personally, had said that the same instructions applied to us.

As soon as I had collected my railway warrant from Southampton to Salisbury I went out on to the platform as a train was about to leave. 'Where is this for?' I asked the guard. 'London', he said so I jumped aboard. As we approached Waterloo I worked my way forward to the front of the train. As soon as it stopped I jumped out and ran towards the barrier as though in a great hurry. I waved my warrant in the direction of the man on the barrier as I ran past him, saying 'I'm on duty', which was at least partly true. He did not stop me. I dived into the Underground, which was still running, and so got home, very late. I had written from France to say that I was due at Larkhill on Thursday and expected to get a weekend pass starting on Friday. In anticipation, Anne had gone to my home, but they had all given up hope of my arrival and gone to bed.

England had not had any of the snow which had blanketed Northern France since Christmas, but it was getting very cold. Anne saw me off on Sunday evening when I caught the train to Salisbury. I thought my warrant (Southampton to Salisbury) would be queried, but it was not. The train made an increasing number of stops and on peering out of the window we saw that it was snowing. Progress was very slow. Midnight came and went and I hoped there would be an early morning bus to get me to Larkhill. We eventually pulled in to Salisbury and found the RTO's office full of troops who had to get to installations on Salisbury Plain. When it became light we were told no buses were running. Eventually some Army lorries arrived, including one for Larkhill. When we got on the road we saw the damage which had been done during the night. The snow was thick and soft. The telephone wires were coated with ice to a thickness of an inch or more. In some places, the weight of this had broken the wires, in others it had pulled the poles down to the ground. At Larkhill, expecting that I was in all sorts of trouble, I reported to the office. The clerk there simply noted that I had arrived and told me to go over to the quartermaster's stores. Here I was issued with blankets and a sergeant took me to where I was to sleep I asked him where the lecture huts were, but he asked 'Haven't you just come over from the BEF?' I said I had. 'You haven't had any breakfast, have you?' I said I had not but that I was overdue for the first lecture. 'Bugger that', he said and took me to the cook-house. He told the sergeant cook that I was just in from the BEF and had had no breakfast. The sergeant told me to sit at a table and gave me a mug of hot, strong, sweet tea, for which I was grateful. He busied himself at the stove and produced a plateful of bacon, sausages, tinned tomatoes and fried bread. Also on the table appeared more bread and butter and marmalade. It was now well past nine o'clock, but I thought I might as well be hanged for a sheep as for a lamb and tucked in.

When I eventually reached the lecture hut, the officer who was lecturing said cheerfully 'Come in, bombardier. Find yourself a seat. We haven't done much. You'll catch up'. I found a seat among the NCOs at the back. I saw that I was only the second from the BEF to arrive. I am afraid that, following a sleepless night and a hearty breakfast, sitting in a hut the warmth of which contrasted with the cold atmosphere outside, I dozed off. Two of my colleagues from France arrived that afternoon, one the following morning and the last one not until that evening. He claimed he had been snowed up in North Wales. Nobody asked why we had not gone directly to Larkhill from Southampton.

The course was interesting. The subjects covered were flash spotting, sound ranging, the interpretation of air photographs and the use of the artillery board. I frankly thought the first two were rather crude. They relied on the observations of a variety of individuals and so were very subject to human error. The interpretation of photographs taken from the air was fascinating.

Suspicious objects had to be identified and clues sought as to where these were, for they were often well hidden. Their precise location had then to be established. This was done by relating them to features whose position was known. An obvious example of this is a church. We were told that the intersection of tracks was more reliable than reference to roads which often changed, whereas tracks had been in the same place for centuries. They showed up well on the photographs, even when they had been ploughed over. A complication arose in that few of the photographs were taken immediately above the area and an ingenious method had been devised to allow for the angle at which they had been taken.

An artillery board is a drawing board the size of a sheet of a 1:25,000 map. It is mounted on a stand and covered with a sheet of cartridge paper on which is printed the same grid as on the map, that is at intervals of one kilometre. Just as when on a car journey sod's law dictates that the road one is following wanders from page to page of the road atlas, so the area to be covered in any artillery operation is rarely confined to one 1:25,000 sheet. It is therefore necessary to make up one's own map and number the grid lines accordingly. For flash spotting and sound ranging, the position of the observers were pin-pointed and angles drawn according to what they saw in the hope that there might be intersections pointing to where the enemy guns were. The board was also used in placing information from air photographs.

The course instructors told us to expect our postings before the end of the course. They did not come through, however, so we were issued with seven-day leave passes and railway warrants to our homes and thence to Dover. We would probably be informed by post of our new postings. No instructions arrived, however, so after a pleasant week at home Anne saw me off to Dover. The concourse at Victoria was a distressing place, with many tearful wives, sweethearts and mothers seeing their loved ones off. Had they realised how bad this was for the troops' morale, they would, I hope, have tried to restrain themselves.

The RTO in Dover told me to go aboard the *Canterbury*, a ferry bound for Boulogne. There I found the other NCOs who were on my course. We were all summoned to the gangway and thought our postings had come through. We were merely told to go on another ferry moored just in front. What difference it made which boat we sailed on I cannot imagine. So I returned to my unit in Armentières.

9

February 1940

The adjutant told me that everyone on my course had been sent back to their units to form a pool from which they could be posted to a Corps HQ when required. In the meantime I was to work in RHQ and act as an operations clerk when the regiment went on exercises. In the RHQ office I found that Lieut. Noton had been appointed Town Major of Armentières and had an office in the Town Hall. Chalky, who had a somewhat relaxed attitude to life, had been moved to a battery and his place had been taken by Tug Wilson. He was a reservist, a tough little Geordie. He had worked for a Newcastle paper and could type at an incredible speed. One of his jobs had been, every Saturday afternoon during the football season, to take down match reports as they were dictated to him over the telephone by reporters. He did this directly on to the typewriter whence the copy went straight to the sub-editors. Accuracy was not so important as speed—it was up to the sub-editors to make any corrections. He had to be much more careful when typing Army orders etc.

My first impression was that he was rough and ready and that we would not have much in common. I changed my opinion when he came in one evening, very morose, having consumed several beers. 'This (several expletives) war', he moaned. 'It's my little lad's first birthday and I should be celebrating it with him and his mum'. He went on to tell me what a great little fellow he was. He then went on to say how lovely his wife was, a virtuous little lady whom he adored. I met her later. She was indeed a very nice girl and not likely to have moved in the same circles as Tug. I wondered how they had ever met. There was no doubt, however, that theirs was a successful marriage, based on mutual affection and respect.

The weather having improved, exercises were frequent. When

we set up a regimental command post, I found that my job was to help the assistant adjutant. I was surprised to find that this was not being done by the sergeant artillery clerk, but he never appeared in the command post. I set up the artillery board and the officer numbered the grid lines. We worked to twelve-figure co-ordinates, which gave positions to the nearest metre. This was somewhat ambitious as we reckoned that the narrowest line we could draw (with a 4H pencil sharpened to a spade point) represented 10 metres on a 1:25,000 map. Still, we did our best with the aid of a magnifying glass. One of us entered information on the board as it came in and the other checked the entry. The first messages came by DR, but the Royal Signals unit laid lines very quickly and were soon taking the messages over the field telephone. We would enter battery command posts, troop positions, observation posts (OPs) and forward observation posts (FOPs). Then the colonel and adjutant would return from a recce and detail defensive fire (DF) and harassing fire (HF) tasks. DF tasks were positions likely to be occupied by the enemy, such as machine gun posts and mortar sites. HF tasks would be bridges and their approaches, crossroads, defiles such as lanes with embankments on each side, in fact anywhere where a random shell might do some damage, the aim being to make life uncomfortable for the enemy. Each task would be given a number so that it could be identified quickly. As soon as these were entered, I had to make tracings of them, which were sent to the batteries. This enabled the troop commanders to work out the range, bearing and elevation of their guns for each task, and the charge to be used. The ammunition for the 25-pounder was called QF Separate. This meant that the projectiles and fuses were packed separately from the brass cartridge cases, which contained three bags of cordite. If all three were used, the weapon operated as a gun. If one or two bags were removed, it had to be fired at a greater elevation to achieve the same range so that it acted as a howitzer. When creeping barrages were agreed with the infantry, I had to do tracings of these for them and the batteries. I found my job interesting and thought it worthwhile.

I resumed my duties as postal orderly. I had a shock one day when driving the truck back to RHQ. I came to a crossroads where I had to turn right. The visibility along the road to my left was poor, due to a bend. This was not helped by driving a vehicle with right hand drive in a country where one had to keep to the right. I saw nothing coming so drove slowly round the corner. At that moment a staff car came from the left and had to swerve to avoid me. It stopped in front of us and its driver signalled to me to stop also. The man whose truck I was driving said happily 'You're for it now'. (I have mentioned previously that the battery drivers hated me driving their precious vehicles.) I did not feel that I was at fault but nevertheless approached the car with apprehension. In the back there were two staff officers, both looking fixedly ahead. I recognised one of them as being the King's brother, the Duke of Gloucester, who was a professional soldier. I saluted and waited for the worst. 'Is this the road to Armentières?' asked their driver. I said it was. 'Thanks mate', he said, and drove off.

The relaxed atmosphere of the town was disturbed one day when a battalion of the Argyll and Sutherland Highlanders arrived. They swept in, wearing their steel helmets, rifles at the ready, as though they were liberating the place. DRs peremptorily held up all traffic as their vehicles roared by. They moved into the central residential area between us and the Green Howards. That evening they invaded some of the Green Howards' watering holes and caused trouble. They were forcibly ejected, some chairs etc. being broken in the process. We expected trouble the following night, but for some reason we were left in peace.

A Divisional Order was received that a venereal disease was regarded as a self-inflicted wound and that any man contracting one would be charged and dealt with severely. Presumably this was a problem in some units but I never heard of a case in mine.

With the improved weather, the padre was able to fulfil his wish to get together a rugby team. He had taken a few of us to watch the French army play the RAF. It was quite a good match but my principal memory of the day is of the bands, which played before it started. The large French band came first, clad in khaki with their metal helmets. They marched at a quick pace, raising their knees much more than we do, their military band in front being answered, as it were, by the bugles at the back. They were followed by one of our Guards' bands, in scarlet jackets and busbies. They marched at their usual steady pace, the music sounding solid and inspiring compared to the reed instruments of the French.

The padre had obtained permission to use a pitch at a technical college, together with its excellent changing and shower facilities. We found after a few practice sessions that we could put out quite a reasonable team. Our first match was to be against the 91st Field Regiment. Formerly the Kent Yeomanry, they were neighbours at home of our 368 Battery based at Woolwich. Both sides had men who played for Blackheath, including one or two who had won Kent county caps. It promised to be a tough match.

One morning I woke up with a headache, a runny nose and a sore throat. I felt rotten so, for the first time I went on sick parade. I was furious when the MO said 'M and D, two aspirins'. M and D stood for medicine and duty, which to me carried a suggestion that I was a malingerer. I went to the office in high dudgeon. During the morning the padre looked into the office. 'Rugger practice this afternoon, Wild. The adjutant says you can come', and disappeared. 'You can't go, of course', said the sergeant. 'You're sick'. 'No I'm not', I replied. 'If I'm fit for duty, I'm fit for rugger'. The sergeant did not argue so, though I knew it to be foolish, I went. My position of flank forward involves continuous activity and I left the field soaked in perspiration. I showered and walking back to HQ I suddenly realised that my head, nose and throat were all back to normal. I concluded that I had sweated out whatever bug had attacked me. I do not suggest that rugby football is the best cure for a cold, but it certainly did me more good than the MO's aspirins.

The regiment had the use of a large hall and ENSA started to send us entertainers every week or so. Unfortunately, the standard was so low that attendances fell off rapidly. This was a pity so far as the entertainers were concerned, for they gave the impression that they thought they were bravely entering a battle zone to boost our morale. They were, after all, in Armentières, a town always associated with the Great War. In fact the war so far was properly described by the newspapers as phoney. Far from dodging shot and shell we mixed happily with the towns-people. We did not carry gas-masks, for instance, because they had none. Attendance at the concerts was no longer voluntary. Each battery and RHQ were given quotas. When a concert took place, men were detailed to attend and were marched to the hall. The last concert I attended was the worst of all. The party had the usual make-up of an end-of-pier show and was led by a tall, white-headed man who told us at the outset that he was proud to be back where he had entertained 'the boys' in the last war. We endured the first half when our visitors confirmed that their jokes were not funny, the vocalists could not sing and their sketches pointless. As soon as the interval started one of the gunners went in front of the stage and launched forth into the song unfolding the plot of many a Victorian melodrama *She wos pore but she was honest*, to the delight of the audience. I had never heard so many verses of the song. There must have been about twenty. After each verse we roared out the chorus in the South London version of Cockney:

> It's the sime the 'ole world over
> It's the pore wot gets the blime,
> While the rich gets all the pleasure.
> Isn't it a bleedin' shime!

It was the best act of the evening. When the song was finished and the soloist sat down, the curtains opened to reveal the old man, clad in shining armour, striking a heroic pose. 'The White Knight', he declaimed and then proceeded to deliver a long monologue. It was heard in silence. When it was ended I felt sorry for the old fellow and started to clap. So few others did, however, that it made the thinness of the applause the more obvious. Undeterred, he said 'Well, boys, I know you all like a sing-song so we'll have one now, starting with that good old favourite of you all, *Pack up your troubles*. There was a universal groan. If there was one song which this generation of soldiers did not sing it was that one. Neither were *Tipperary* or *Roses of Picardy* or any of the songs their fathers sang. They would bellow out *South of the border down Mexico way*, *Roll out the barrel*, *She'll be coming round the mountain* or *Nellie Dee* with gusto. Still more popular were Army songs, the first lines of which (expurgated where necessary) were *Bless 'em all*, *They call it bravery on the field*, *When this bloomin' war is over* (sung to the tune of *What a friend we have in Jesus*) and *We are Fred Karno's army* (sung to the tune of *The Church's one foundation*).

I doubt whether the old fellow knew any of these and the White Knight would certainly not have tolerated the bad language of the Army songs, but he ploughed on, without getting any response from the conscripted audience. 'Come on boys', he said. 'Play the game. You know you all used to like singing the grand old songs.' The poor chap had not a clue. He was no doubt an enthusiastic volunteer, but whoever sent him to France must have been completely devoid of imagination.

Relief from ENSA came at the beginning of April when it was announced that at the end of the month the Division would be withdrawn from its positions on the Belgian border for three weeks. The first week was to be spent in recreation, with as little work done as possible. In the second week there was to be unit training and in the third divisional exercises would take place. There was also to be a cross-country race for which each unit would put in a team of six. A cross-country race was organised for the regiment to choose its team. Some of my friends and I did not want to be in the team, not relishing the training which would be involved. We therefore kept together from the start, jogging along comfortably whilst others dashed on ahead. We did not pass any of them, so were surprised when we came to the finish to be told that we would be the team. The blighters who had gone ahead of us had skived off somewhere and left us to win. I gave up smoking cigarettes.

I had found the soft cheeses produced in that part of France very much to my liking so I decided, before leaving Armentières, to send Anne some samples. I found a cardboard box and packed it with as many varieties as it would hold and posted it to her. I am told that when the postman delivered the parcel he was holding it at arm's length. It had during its transit to England evidently been kept in warm surroundings and the effect was, to put it mildly, pungent.

We moved south on 29 April, passing through towns associated with the previous war: La Bassée, Béthune, Saint-Pol, Doullens and Amiens. We arrived eventually at Lihus, in the Oise department. RHQ took up residence in the barns of a well-kept farm. After settling in we began our promised week of rest. Different men used the time in different ways. Some seemed to want only to sleep. The drinkers were out of luck because the only beverage sold in the village estaminet, apart from coffee, was the local red wine and it tasted horrible. We had some fun. In the farmyard were several turkeys — large, ugly creatures. One of our drivers had a tall, lean figure, a long neck and a prominent Adam's apple. He would stand in front of the biggest and ugliest turkey, which ruled the flock with a rod of iron, lean forward, stretch out his neck and literally gobble at it. The bird evidently saw this as a challenge and would gobble back ferociously. It was extremely funny, especially as the turkey recognised the driver whenever he passed by and immediately issued a spirited challenge.

The people of the village were friendly and made us feel welcome. It was a tranquil place and the possibility that hostilities might break out at any time seemed remote. One morning there was a procession to the church of children about seven or eight years of age. Walking two by two, the little girls wore white dresses and the boys white shirts and dark trousers. They were going to their first communion. It was a charming sight.

I went for walks. It was sunny and warm and the Picardy countryside was pleasant after the comparatively drab and uninteresting north. I found a wood which was carpeted with cowslips and violets. Anne and I had often visited the bluebell woods of Surrey on our tandem rides, but I had never seen such a wonderful wood as this. I gathered some of the flowers, wrapped them in a couple of dock leaves and posted them to Anne, hoping they would at least be recognisable when they arrived.

The Germans had invaded Scandinavia during April and now the news from Norway was not good. We heard that the 15th Infantry Brigade had been sent there as reinforcements. The 15th was 'our' brigade, the infantry with whom we operated on exercises. There was speculation that we might join them. I went on an errand to the CRA's HQ at Beauvais, hoping to get some information from the clerks there, but without success.

On Friday 10 May the Germans invaded the Low Countries. The phoney war was over. It was ironic that after sitting on the Belgian frontier for seven months, ready for action at any time, we should find ourselves withdrawn from the line and in reserve. Still, we were grateful for our brief period of relaxation. It helped to set us up for what was to come.

PART TWO : ACTION

1

Friday 10 May 1940

Between the wars France had constructed a line of fortifications along its border from Basle in Switzerland to Longwy where the border of France meets those of Luxembourg and Belgium. Known as the Maginot Line, this was thought to be impregnable and in fact it was never breached. North of the end of the line lay the Ardennes and the French military experts were of the opinion that no invading army, especially one relying on the use of tanks, could penetrate its forested hills and valleys. Beyond this was the Belgian border, but as France was bound under treaty to defend Belgium if it was attacked, there was no point in constructing permanent defences with Belgium in front of them. When France and Britain went to war with Germany, Belgium declared neutrality so our forces could not enter the country. The BEF and two French armies were therefore stationed along the border ready to enter Belgium if need be.

As soon as the news arrived of the German invasion of the Low Countries, the Divisional programme for the remainder of our three weeks' 'rest' was abandoned and we prepared for action. The first task was to get rid of excess baggage. All except our basic kit, together with personal items, was packed into our kitbags, to which labels were attached with our home addresses and they were despatched. Vehicles and guns were given rigorous maintenance inspections and everything made ready for a rapid move.

The news from the front was bad from the outset and it soon got worse. The RAF in France consisted of some Hurricane fighters and some Blenheim bombers. Many planes were

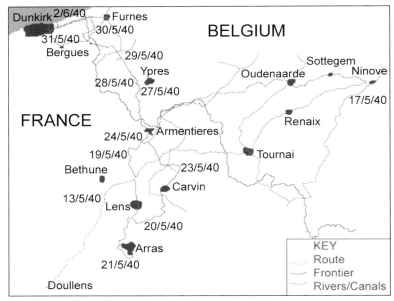

7 Overall map of action in France and Belgium, May 1940.

destroyed on the ground in the first onslaught. Most of the remaining bombers sacrificed themselves in a brave but unsuccessful attempt to bomb the Meuse bridges. The Hurricanes gave a good account of themselves but they were totally inadequate to deal with the numbers of planes, which the Germans were able to put into action. So from those early days the BEF was without air cover. On 12 May the Germans crossed the Meuse.

Meanwhile, our regiment was switched temporarily into the 50th (Northumbrian) Division. This made sense, for the 5th Division, having lost the 15th Infantry Brigade, had a field artillery regiment (us) with no specific operational function. The 50th Division had its quota of field artillery regiments, but they were still equipped with 18-pounder guns and 4.5 inch howitzers. Our 25-pounders, with their versatility, longer range and heavier projectiles, could increase the division's firepower considerably. So we moved to Hersin-Coupigny, a village in the coal mining area between Lens and Béthune, to join our new division.

Every vehicle carried two removable signs. One denoted the formation to which it belonged, the other its unit number within that formation. Work started immediately to change our signs. The 'Y' of the 5th Division had to be replaced with the 'TT' (for Tyneside Territorials) of the 50th. This was a big job to be done quickly. To help us out the artillery regiment in our new division which had the same number as us volunteered to change their number. This saved at least a day.

On 14 May the French line was breached at Sedan, out-flanking the Maginot Line. The following day, Holland capitulated. The next afternoon I typed my first operation order. The regiment was to move, independently of the division, into Belgium.

2

Friday 17 May 1940

We set off early on Friday morning, crossing the frontier at Baisieux. As we went through Tournai the town was quiet, though there were menacing sounds of aircraft not far away. Not long afterwards the whole area suffered a devastating air attack. We went on through Renaix. The road was empty, the weather was lovely and the pleasant countryside peaceful. We finally went into a 'hide' in an orchard near Nederbrakel. The cooks served a meal of the usual stew, after which the RSM paraded the men of RHQ. He then told us we were about to enter a battle zone and harangued us as to our conduct there. We were, he said, to wear our steel helmets at all times except when under cover. Any man who did not do so would be put on a charge and dealt with severely. 'Put them on now', he ordered, so we all obediently donned our 'battle bowlers'.

We were soon on the move again. The Regimental Command Post was set up in a large house in the village of Oitre. We unloaded the things we needed from the office truck, which was then sent back to the wagon lines. To my surprise, the sergeant artillery clerk announced that he was going with it. The officers seemed not to object, so he went and did not appear in the command post for the rest of the campaign. So Tug and I were left to cope.

Meanwhile, the colonel and adjutant had gone to reconnoitre the area we would be covering and deciding with the battery commanders and their observation officers the siting of OPs and troop positions. I busied myself with the artillery board as messages began to come in, just as I had done on repeated exercises. The 2 i/c had gone to supervise the wagon lines and Lieut. Marsh, the assistant adjutant, had been called away, so Tug and I were alone in the office. This was in a large room at

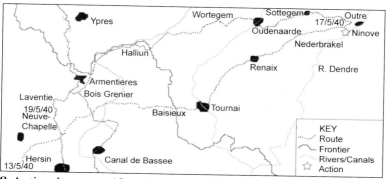

8 Action between 13 and 19 May 1940.

the back of the house, which had a large window overlooking a field, about the size of two football pitches, probably a paddock. It had a thick hedge down each side and across the end. I was working in front of the window when I heard an aeroplane engine. I looked up in time to see a biplane, painted khaki, flying quite slowly a few feet above the hedge on my right. It banked to fly along the bottom hedge, displaying two large black crosses on its wings. 'It's one of theirs', Tug said. I suddenly realised that the work I had been doing so mechanically was for real and not merely an exercise. I grabbed the message forms with which I had dealt from Tug, who was filing them, and checked every entry I had made. I realised that from now on accuracy on my part was an essential ingredient for the efficiency of the regiment.

During the short night little happened so far as Tug and I were concerned. The batteries, however, as soon as darkness fell, moved up into their troop positions. Gun pits were dug and guns in position and vehicles returned to the wagon lines before first light. 365 Battery was deployed round the village of Nederhasselt on our left and 368 Battery round Aspelaaere on our right, along the ridge above the river Dendre. I knew the situation from typing operation orders and from what Lieut. Marsh had told me. The advancing Germans had broken through the French line on the Somme and the British divisions, in danger of being out-flanked, had to withdraw round Brussels to establish a new

defence line along the river Escaut. This involved crossing the
river Dendre and a rearguard, consisting of the 25th Infantry
Brigade and the 3rd Battalion of the Grenadier Guards, was to
cover the withdrawal and to guard the bridges over the Dendre,
in or near Ninove. Our task was to supply the firepower for this
rearguard.

As soon as it was light the CO went out surveying the ground
we were to cover with the Battery commanders and observation
officers. Our positions along the ridge were ideal so far as
observation was concerned. The whole area of operations was to
be seen clearly in the light of a beautiful day. Targets could be
identified and their exact locations determined with comparative
ease. The CO ordered alternative OPs and a forward observation
post (FOP) was even set up on the far side of the river. Information poured in all day for addition to the artillery board. Meanwhile the main force was withdrawing in good order along the
main roads on each side of us. All day the regiment was waiting,
poised for action but it was not until 7 p.m. that we were ordered
to fire. From that time on it seemed that all hell was let loose.
There seemed to be no pause when none of our troops was
firing. It seemed that we were to put over as much fire as
possible to give the enemy the impression that the strength of our
artillery was more than one unit.

All night the CO directed operations on the field telephone
giving orders when the infantry asked for particular targets to be
engaged. I realised then and in the days to come what a fine man
he was. Lieut.-Col. C.B. Wood, who was a dental surgeon by
profession, had won the Military Cross whilst serving in the
regiment as a subaltern in the First World War. He was always
calm and decisive, never flustered. He did his best for the
welfare of his men but did not hesitate to demand of them
supreme effort when he deemed it necessary. The Battery
commanders kept him informed of important happenings. On one
occasion it was reported that the infantry commander had
requested fire on a target which was known to be within yards of
the position of some of his own troops. He was told of the
danger of even a slight inaccuracy, but he said that it was

necessary because the men had been cut off by the enemy from one of the bridgeheads. A few minutes later the call came in—the firing had been successful. There was alarm for some time because the officer and his assistants in the FOP were missing. They turned up eventually having stayed at their post so long that they were nearly cut off.

At about 6 a.m. the first of the rearguard came back As they passed through the lines of F Troop a platoon of Guards raised three cheers for the gunners. This spontaneous gesture from some of the world's finest soldiers did wonders for the morale of the regiment.

At 9 a.m. the order was issued to cease fire. In fourteen hours our twenty-four guns had between them fired off over three thousand rounds. Keeping them supplied with ammunition had been a headache for the quartermaster. He had appeared several times in the command post to report progress to the colonel, but he was able to locate supplies when they were needed. So ended our first action against the enemy. We had not come under fire ourselves and no casualties had been reported.

Shortly after the ceasefire, the order was issued to prepare to move. It did not come too soon, for one of the batteries reported that they had come under fire from enemy guns using shrapnel. The Germans had brought up their artillery very quickly. Fortunately the troop concerned was able to get its guns and trailers hitched up and removed from the gun site whilst only ranging rounds were coming over and once again there were no casualties.

3

Sunday 19 May 1940

I had read the movement order over Tug's shoulder as he typed it. We were to proceed via Sottegem and Oudenaarde to Wortegem on the far side of the Escaut, where we were to take up defensive positions. As we neared Oudenaarde, the road we were following climbed steadily up the left hand side of a broad valley. Another road ran along the top of the other side of the valley. This was crammed with refugees. There were lorries piled high with household goods, cars on top of which mattresses had been tied, perambulators and bicycles and pedestrians carrying loads as best they could.

A large formation of Stuka dive-bombers appeared. They were the first Stukas we had seen. In our battle position enemy aircraft had appeared, two or three at a time and some groups of our men had been fired at, without suffering any casualties. There must have been a light AA battery not far away because we occasionally heard the pop-pop-pop of the 40 mm Bofors guns. A farmhouse nearby had been bombed for no obvious reason.

The Stukas flew in a large V-shaped formation. There must have been twenty or thirty of them. We pulled into what cover was offered by trees lining the road and halted. The bombers ignored us, though a regiment of artillery strung out over six miles of road must have been visible to them. They concentrated their attention on the helpless refugees. Two or three at a time, they peeled off from their formation and dived on their prey. The scream of the engines was reinforced by sirens carried on the wings. They machine-gunned the slow-moving column, for which no cover was available, and dropped the occasional small anti-personnel bomb. This was a massacre of a crowd of civilians, mostly women and children, the citizens of a country which had declared itself neutral but which Germany had nevertheless

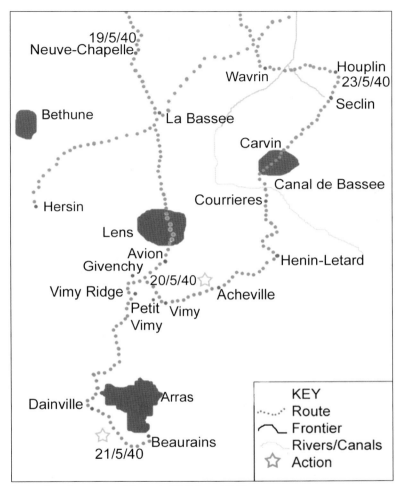

9 Action between 19 and 23 May 1940.

invaded. The only possible motive was to spread terror and blind panic leading to a confusion which might impede our forces.

We expected such atrocities from the Nazis. Some people, however, would have had us believe that these consisted only of a wicked few. The German race, we were told, was cultured and civilised. This atrocity was being carried out by the Luftwaffe, proud professionals, the pilots of which formed an elite, the flower of German youth, of which the whole country was proud. It was obvious that, though the Nazis might be the worst, the German forces were ruthless and would stop at nothing to gain their ends. Any regrets I had for the death and injury of those on the receiving end of our gunfire disappeared.

From then on we saw Stukas daily, in huge formations—on one occasion I counted fifty. We learned that we were safe so long as they kept in formation. When two or three started to peel off, it was advisable to take cover.

On this occasion one of the planes got its come-uppance. After its deadly run over the refugees, it veered left down the slope of the valley and up our side. As it crossed the road ahead of us there was a burst of fire from a Bren gun, followed by a crash and explosion up the hill to our left. When we reached the crossroads, we found a motorcyclist from the Northumberland Fusiliers dancing around like a dervish shouting 'Got the bastard'. He had a Bren gun mounted on his sidecar and had scored a lucky hit as the plane flew a few feet over him. At the top of the hill was a pillar of flame and smoke.

We moved on through the countryside, which was quiet and pleasant in the beautiful weather except for the bombers polluting the sky from time to time. Oudenaarde, when it came into sight, was an attractive town nestling in the Escaut valley. We passed through it and across the river. We had not gone far before there was the tumult of a heavy air raid behind us. It started just as 368 Battery, at the rear of the column, was about to enter the town. Immediately the raid was over the Battery did so, to find a scene of utter devastation. When they reached the bridge, they found it destroyed and had to proceed along the river-bank until they found another and joined the rest of the regiment at Wortegem.

We went into hides and, after a meal settled down for a much needed rest. Hardly had we done so when I was hauled out to type an operation order. I assumed this would be for us to move to battle positions guarding the Escaut. It was a shock therefore, to read that the 92nd Field Regiment, with a battery of light AA and a company of Field Engineers, all under the command of Lieut.-Col. Wood, was to go back into France with the task of holding the line of the La Bassée Canal for as long as possible. Not much more than an hour later we started our journey.

The journey was a nightmare. Everyone was still tired and orders were issued that passengers in the cabs of vehicles must stay awake and make sure that the drivers did not doze. I had to pinch myself to keep from nodding off. The only light on every vehicle was a small spotlight under the rear, which shone on the differential, which had been painted white. Every driver had to keep his eyes on the dim light of the vehicle in front and the effect was hypnotic. The first part of our route lay along country lanes but when we reached a major road we found it more and more encumbered with refugees, who posed an additional hazard.

As we were nearing Halluin, where we were to cross the frontier, the 2 i/c, who was leading the convoy, the colonel having gone on ahead, led us along a lane, which branched off to the left. We assumed he had found a way of avoiding the refugees. The lane was unmetalled and got bumpier as we went along. Suddenly, to our horror, we found ourselves in a farm-yard, the only access to which was the lane along which we had come. Extricating the vehicles from that narrow lane in the pitch dark was tiresome, to put it mildly. Fortunately only RHQ trucks were involved. Had there been any guns, with their trailers, to turn round in it would have been virtually impossible.

So we rejoined the main road. The crowd got thicker and thicker until we finally inched our way across the frontier. The road got clearer. We passed through Armentières which was quiet in the darkness, then on through Bois-Grenier and Laventie. By the time we reached Neuve-Chappelle it was light. The RHQ trucks were parked in the forecourt leading to the parish church. It was opposite the famous crucifix, which stood unscathed in the First World War when the village round about it was flattened by shellfire.

The cooks made us a very acceptable brew of tea and we settled down for a much needed rest whilst waiting for the colonel to return.

4

Monday 20 May 1940

When the colonel arrived, he called an officers' briefing. As soon as this was over, we were ordered to mount. (The artillery has never forgotten that it traditionally relied on the horse for transport.) The colonel led us south to La Bassée where, to my surprise, we crossed the canal. We went on through Lens until we saw before us Vimy Ridge, with the great cleft pillar of the Canadian War Memorial dominating the landscape. We ascended the road leading up to the ridge and halted when we came to the top. I walked the few yards to the crest of the hill. From here one could see a long way. The countryside looked peaceful with no signs of war, though I knew that a fierce battle had been raging in Arras, which must have been only just out of sight.

In front of me the Royal Engineers were advancing in line abreast down the hill, their rifles at the ready. This cannot have been the role they expected to fill when they were ordered to accompany us. I presumed that this was to destroy the bridges over the canal if necessary. As I watched them I thought of the 'thin red line' and reflected that here we had a very thin khaki line and hoped it would not be long before they were replaced by infantry in force. I expect they hoped so too.

There was a group of cottages nearby and we were ordered to set up a command post in one of them. The inhabitants had left in a great hurry. In some of the kitchens the remains of a meal remained on the table. Whilst Tug and I took the equipment we needed into our chosen cottage, the others investigated the other buildings, probably in search of food, for our rations were getting short. They were unlucky, but what they did find was that every cottage had outbuildings in which there were chickens and rabbits in small cages. They had been abandoned without food or water. We thought the most humane thing to do was to open the doors of the cages to set them free to fend for themselves, so that is what we did. Tug and I had hardly finished our task when we were told to load up again. The colonel had decided to set up the regimental command post in a large country house a mile or so away down the hill, on the outskirts of Givenchy. 365 Battery was deployed just below the ridge near the hamlet of Petit-Vimy and 368 Battery near Avion, just north of Givenchy.

We found our new HQ palatial. The house stood in extensive grounds and was approached by a drive. The rooms were large and there was plenty of space for everybody. RHQ officers were billeted in rooms on the upper floor. When we had set up the office we explored the ground floor and found below it a wine cellar. Realising that we were part of a desperate attempt to slow down the German advance, we thought it our duty to 'liberate' some before Jerry got it. We could not drink much, of course, because we needed to keep our wits about us, but I found a bottle of wine, which was very palatable. It went down well with the army biscuits, which had replaced bread in our rations for over a week. These biscuits were so hard they had to be nibbled and allowed to moisten in one's mouth to a consistency which it was possible to swallow.

Large formations of bombers of various types flew over us continually. They paid no attention to us. They were obviously bent on pounding Arras and beyond. We also became aware of a reconnaissance plane, which we saw for hours at a time from then on. It was an ugly contraption, not unlike our own Lysander but far more angular. We called it, rightly or wrongly, a 'Stork'. It must have taken enough photographs of us in the course of a couple of weeks to fill a small gallery. I could visualise the German counter-battery clerks poring over them to establish the precise positions of our guns, command posts and wagon lines.

During the evening and the early part of the night a brigade of infantry took up positions below the ridge. Our observation officers on the ridge reported that there was no sign of the enemy on the terrain in front of them, though there were the sounds of battle in Arras, just out of view to the left. When darkness fell the sky over Arras was illuminated by fires and flashes, whilst beyond Arras what were presumed to be German rockets signalling successes appeared.

Not long after midnight, the colonel and the adjutant went to Brigade HQ. When they returned, the two battery commanders were summoned to a briefing meeting. The Germans, still held up by the Welsh Guards in Arras, had advanced south of the town and were pressing westwards in an attempt to reach the Channel coast. They now held a corridor some twenty miles wide. A two-pronged attack was to take place to cut this corridor. At the same time the French were supposed to attack it from the south.

The attack was to be made by two battalions of infantry advancing along parallel roads. Each battalion was to be supported by one of our batteries, which would be under the command of the battalion commander. When the objective had been achieved, a brigade command post would be established and our colonel would set up a regimental command post.

At mid morning our batteries left their positions and advanced over the ridge, 368 Battery to the left and 365 Battery to the right. We packed up ready to follow them when called upon to set up the new command post. Meanwhile, the colonel, with the adjutant, went forward, doing all he could to keep in touch with both the batteries.

All day we waited to be called forward. We had no idea how the operation was faring. It must be remembered that in those days there was no radio as we know it today. The batteries had cumbersome 'wireless' equipment, which had a very short range. Field telephones were our quickest means of communication, but these could only come into use when the situation was sufficiently static for land lines to be laid. Otherwise we had to rely on messages, usually carried by DR.

Having nothing else to do we spent all day in the garden, enjoying the sunshine. At about midday we saw, coming from the east along the road just below the ridge, a column of refugees. Where they thought they were going is a mystery, but the civilian population by now were in such a panic that all they wanted to do was to flee anywhere. As we watched one of the large formations of Stukas which had been passing over us all the morning decided to take an interest in them. As in Belgium, they machine-gunned and bombed their helpless targets mercilessly. We could do nothing about it. We reflected that the 365 Battery gun positions were near that road, so that there was at least the consolation that going forward had spared them a strafing.

In the late afternoon we had news. The colonel's DR brought a message that the attack had failed and that the regiment was to come back to its former positions. We set up the command post again. When the colonel returned he looked grim. We gradually found out why. The operation had initially had some success. British light tanks, with a motorcycle unit and some French cuirassiers, had intercepted a German column after the Panzers had passed and played havoc with motorised infantry following up. Advanced elements of our own infantry rounded up about four hundred prisoners and marched them back. Later, however, the infantry came up against some heavy tanks and were forced to withdraw and eventually abandon the operation.

The colonel, and the battery commanders when they returned, were annoyed because they considered our batteries had not been used properly by the infantry. They had practised this sort of operation with the 15th Infantry Brigade and knew what sort of support they could give. The battalion commanders under whose command they had been today seemed to have no idea how to use the guns. In the first place, both batteries had difficulty making contact with the infantry commanders. When they did so 365 Battery was not called into action at all. The colonel contacted by 368 Battery eventually decided that it would be useful for some bridges over a river about four miles ahead to be shelled.

To reach its allotted gun positions the battery had to pass through Dainville, south of Arras. As they did so, the town came under heavy bombardment from the air and from shelling. It was here the regiment suffered its first fatality, when a sergeant was struck by a shell splinter and killed instantly. The battery was otherwise unscathed. Hardly had it gone into action, however, than infantry came straggling back past them. They had come up against the heavy German tanks. It had occurred to nobody to warn the artillery of this, so that they were left without infantry cover. They withdrew successfully but were concerned that an observation officer and his assistants had been left high and dry in Beaurains. Somehow, word was got to him of the withdrawal and he and his men eventually managed to get back safely, but they could not bring his truck with its wireless equipment, which had to be destroyed.

365 Battery had a horrible experience when they returned to their positions at Petit-Vimy. They found their gun pits and slit trenches full of corpses. Many of the refugees had apparently taken shelter from the Stukas on the gun sites and had been slain there mercilessly. The survivors had left them where they lay. The battery commander put it to the colonel that it was not practicable to clear away the corpses before putting the guns into position and the colonel told him to establish new positions in Avion, near the other battery.

The next day passed comparatively uneventfully. We were concerned when notification was received that the RASC was to set up a POL (petrol, oil and lubricants) point at coordinates which proved to be at the end of our drive. The supplies were carried in a number of vehicles, the petrol in four gallon disposable cans. Whilst the supply point was operating vehicles from all the units within reach would come to collect what they needed. These would inevitably attract the attention of the Stork, which was the last thing we wanted. The colonel protested to Division HQ, but it was too late. In the event, there was an air raid on Givenchy but at the other end of the town.

The usual large formations of bombers passed over us going south and behind us Lens was bombed heavily. They seemed to ignore us, though we were in full view of the Stork, which stooged around just out of small arms range. The light AA unit had disappeared—rumour had it that it had been knocked out. There was no sign of the enemy to the south, where our troops were still holding out in Arras. The German encircling movement had, however, progressed and our guns fired on targets on Mont-Saint-Éloi and on the plain to the south-west. That day, we went onto half-rations. These amounted to a packet of biscuits each and a small tin of corned beef between two. I was interested to read later, in a book written by one of the battery officers who was sent to establish an OP on the ridge: 'Swallowing a few mouthfuls of fried bully beef, I packed a tin of sardines, some bread, and a bottle of vin rouge for future use, and departed for the ridge'. On his return in the evening he records: 'Veal cutlets, tinned peas, cheddar cheese and vin rouge awaited me at the Command Post. In the circumstances, a Ritzian repast'. Too true it was! His mess must have been carrying very ample supplies.

5

Thursday 23 May 1940

Things were lively the next day from first light. Targets to the west and south-west were down to as little as 2,000 yards. On one occasion the colonel, having met the infantry brigadier, spotted a formation of tanks on Mont-Saint-Éloi and ordered the nearest battery to engage them, enforcing their withdrawal.

In the late afternoon someone rushed into the room we were using as a command post and said 'There are tanks up on the ridge'. We rushed out into the garden and one of the officers looked at them through binoculars. 'It's all right', he said, 'they're French'. 'Yes', said another, 'but what the hell are they doing there?' These were the small tanks of the French DLM— the light mechanised division, which was holding the ridge to the right of our sector. Obviously the right flank was crumbling and the position of our batteries was becoming vulnerable. The colonel summoned the battery commanders and ordered them to move to new positions to the east. He also told us to prepare to move.

We packed up and our cooks brewed up some tea. They seemed to have an inexhaustible supply of tea, condensed milk and sugar and this played a great part in keeping us going. We took the tea into the garden, to a secluded spot just outside the house, where there were some benches. As we chatted, a line of bullet holes appeared along the wall of the house a couple of feet above head height. Our spot was not as secluded as we had thought, so we moved quickly round the corner of the house before the machine-gunner adjusted his range. We learned later that the colonel had also been sniped at in that part of the garden.

The French armoured vehicles continued to crawl along the road up on the ridge. A division's vehicles take a long time to pass, especially when moving at a snail's pace, even when travelling nose to tail, and heaven knew how many troops were in front of them. At last the numbers on the road dwindled. The colonel had received orders from Division to withdraw to Houplin, about thirty miles north. This was the only possible direction in which to go. The enemy's main advance was from the east and we were under attack from south and west. We moved off, up to the ridge road then eastward through the village of Vimy. We had gone less than three miles, however, before we were brought to a halt once more. The traffic ahead seemed immovable. We had arrived at a crossroads in the hamlet of La Gueule d'Ours. Our office truck halted opposite some houses, the next truck on the far side of the crossroads. This was an open 15 cwt, on which was mounted a Bren gun. This was the pitifully inadequate anti-aircraft protection for Regimental HQ. It was manned by Lance-Bombardier George and Gunner Fortune, who had both been members of the regiment for some years. They loved that gun, keeping it in pristine condition and taking their duties seriously. They practised, for instance, changing magazines as quickly as possible and became very proficient.

Lieut. Marsh emerged from the side entrance to the house opposite which my truck was standing and told me to open a temporary office in the kitchen of the house. We had a large metal box in which we kept the latest nominal rolls, acquittance rolls, war diary etc., together with message pads, writing and typing paper, pens and pencils and ink. I grabbed this and took it to the kitchen. I found this clean and tidy with, as I expected, a good table and chairs, so that there was no need to bring in our own. As I laid out the message pads and pencils, I heard the sound of heavy aircraft engines approaching, together with random rifle shots. I went outside to see what was happening. The planes were now very close, their machine guns firing continuously. I heard our Bren gun open up, then there were two soft crumps as two bombers passed the end of the side entrance where I stood. They were flying very low, the nearer one only a few feet immediately above the line of vehicles. The sound of the engines grew fainter, still accompanied by rifle fire, and I went back into the house.

Some minutes later a sergeant-major from the battery following us in the convoy came in, his face grim. 'I've been told to see to things', he said. 'Why?' I asked. 'What's happened?' 'A3 has been bombed. Gunner Fortune is dead and I don't think Bombardier George will live', he replied. I now realised that those two soft crumps were small bombs. 'George has been evacuated by the field ambulance', he added, 'but there isn't much hope for him. He has a terrible wound in the chest.' I had no idea that there was a field ambulance so near us in the convoy.

'I've brought Fortune's things', the BSM said. He produced a pay book and an identity tag. We wore two such tags on string round our necks. They had, crudely stamped on them, our name, regimental number and religion. They were tied in such a way that one could be cut off without disturbing the other. The drill when a man was killed was to forward his pay book and disc to RA Records, together with personal effects and a detailed description of where the body lay. 'How about personal effects?' I asked. The BSM produced a small bag of items which he had taken from the other breast pocket. Fortune's body had been terribly mutilated—I have no intention of going into details—and these items were drenched with his blood. There were a couple of letters, now almost indecipherable. 'It would break someone's heart to get these back. What do you think?' said the sergeant major. There was no officer present to ask and a decision had be made urgently because we could be moving again at any time. 'Do you think this would be the best thing to do?' he nodded towards the range fire, which was still alight. I agreed and the letters were consigned to the flames.

We then came to a number of snapshots. Most of them were indelibly stained with blood and they followed the letters into the range. We were left with three pictures of different girls. 'Do you know who these are?' asked the BSM. I did not. I knew Fortune had a 'best girl' at home, but not what she looked like. He was the sort who quickly made friends with local families wherever we were stationed and he obviously collected photographs, especially those of young women. What if his girlfriend found that he was carrying the pictures of two, or even three, girls strange to her? We came to a quick decision and destroyed the last three. We may not have complied with the book, but we felt it was up to us to minimise the distress of his family and friends.

I visited Fortune's grave a few years ago. It is in a First World War cemetery shared between the French, the British and the Germans, in two long rows of the graves of men who fell in the short campaign of 1940. George's body was never found. His name is inscribed on the memorial in the British cemetery in Dunkirk.

We were soon on the road again. We made fair progress through Acheville, but caught up with the rear of the other traffic and slowed to a crawl. By the time we reached the urban area of Henin-Letard it was dark, but we could see that it had been heavily bombed. In Courrières we crossed the La Bassée canal. I learned later that this was the only bridge over the canal which the Germans had not destroyed. Had they bombed this one we would have been well and truly in the bag.

In the centre of Carvin the road broadened to form a square. As we passed through, we saw that on the opposite side of the square a convent school had been destroyed. On the road in front had been laid in row after row the bodies of girls who had been killed, each one wrapped in a white sheet and perfectly spaced one from the other. There were sixty of them, laid out lovingly in perfect order.

When we reached Seclin, we found that, like the other towns, it had been bombed mercilessly. It was now daylight and we were conscious of the vulnerability to air attack of the great column of British and French vehicles crawling nose to tail. Our apprehension increased when the Stork appeared. We were relieved when we turned left off the main Lille road into the village of Houplin. So ended one of the most distressing days of my life.

6

Friday 24 May 1940

In Houplin we went into hides and were able to get some much-needed rest. The day, however, was not without incident. The Stork had evidently observed our entering the village, which had not up to then been bombed. Now a brief but savage raid took place. One of the batteries reported that a driver had been killed. A little later came the news that the RAOC officer commanding our Light Aid Detachment had also died. This was particularly sad because, not only was he a popular man, but his wife had only a month or two before given birth to their first child. Regimental HQ had now suffered more losses than either of the batteries.

We were warned that reliable reports had been received that German parachutists were thought to have landed in the vicinity. One of the batteries reported that stray small-arms shots had been heard nearby and that a search party had been sent out to investigate, but nothing suspicious had been found.

We set off in the early morning, travelling westwards, I was happy to note, because there was a reliable rumour that the enemy had occupied Seclin, only a short distance to the east, and had already brought up his artillery. We went cross-country through Wavrin then, crossing the route which had taken us only a few days before to Vimy, through Bois-Grenier to Fleurbaix. RHQ was established on a farm near the village which I knew well as I had often walked there during the evening from Armentières, with a friend from RHQ. We would share a litre of bière blonde before walking back. The batteries went into 'hides' in the surrounding area.

Tug and I were fairly busy, catching up with some of the routine tasks which had been neglected in the activity of the past few days. For one thing the adjutant had to get an up-to-date Part

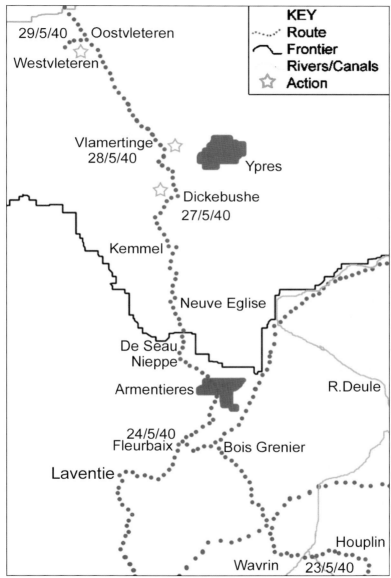

KEY
- Route
- Frontier
- Rivers/Canals
- Action

29/5/40 Oostvleteren
Westvleteren

Vlamertinge
28/5/40
Ypres

Dickebushe
27/5/40

Kemmel

Neuve Eglise

De Seau
Nieppe

Armentieres
R.Deule

24/5/40
Fleurbaix
Bois Grenier

Laventie

Houplin

Wavrin 23/5/40

10 Action between 23 and 29 May 1940.

H Orders issued. Part H Orders contained everything relating to the personnel of the unit—postings, promotions, casualties, courses etc.

For some hours there passed along the road at the bottom of the farm an apparently endless stream of the armoured vehicles of the DLM, going south. The tanks looked absurdly small. Furthermore about one in four was being towed. It was not an impressive sight.

The Stork stooged around as usual and it was joined by a low-flying bomber from which emerged what appeared to be a brilliant ray of light. As it fell we saw that the 'ray' was a cloud of leaflets reflecting the sun. Orders were to collect and destroy them, but not many did. I have my copy to this day. It reads as follows:

British soldiers!
Germans around! You are encircled!

German troupes invaded Courtrai, Tournai, Valenciennes! Lillers, Aire, Saint Omer are occupied. Calais will be taken immediately.

Why do you fight further?

Do you really believes the nonsens that Germans kill their prisonners? Come and see for yourselves the contrary!

The match is finished! A fair ennemy will be fairly treated!

We found the leaflets amusing. Apart from the spelling mistakes, the idea of German 'troupes' suggested that they might be threatening us with their version of ENSA. As for the invitation to see for ourselves whether they killed their 'prisonners', what if it were not 'nonsens' after all?

We were not so amused to hear that the King had called for a National Day of prayer on our behalf. It made us realise that the situation was so dangerous that the Government, contrary to its usual practice, especially in war, had decided to tell the British public the truth, or some of it, thus preparing it for a probable disaster. It did our morale no good at all.

Huge formations of bombers continued to fly over us, mostly from the east. We heard continuing heavy raids to the north, in the direction of Armentières. The town was probably receiving a severe pounding.

When the work slackened off, Tug and I took it in turns to stand by in the office. Just before midnight, when I was on duty, the colonel and adjutant returned from Divisional HQ, to which they had been summoned for a briefing. They at once started drafting a long and detailed operation order for me to type. We were to take part in a large-scale attack to the south, to cut the corridor which the Germans had established to the coast. At the same time the French in the Somme area would attack from the south. Our attack was to be led by the French DLM. (Lord help us! I thought). Stand-to was to be a little before first light, at 3.30, the same as the previous day. It was about 1 a.m. when I finished typing and I was absolutely flaked. The adjutant said to me 'You had better get some rest. I'll get hold of Wilson if we need anything else'.

I went to the barn where RHQ were sleeping, took my boots off, wrapped myself in a blanket and went into a deep sleep.

7

Monday 27 May 1940

It seemed only minutes later that my shoulder was being shaken vigorously by one of our drivers. 'Get cracking, you lazy sod', he said in his usual elegant fashion. 'If you want any breakfast you've got to get over to the cookhouse now'. I sat up and rubbed my eyes. The barn door was wide open and I could see that outside it was bathed in sunshine. 'What's the time?' I asked. 'About seven', he said. 'But stand-to was supposed to be at 3.30'. 'So they say', he replied, 'but whatever it was for has been called off. They rousted us out at six'.

Rations were so short that no meal must ever be missed. I went to the cookhouse, which was in fact in the open air, where the sergeant cook was busy with the frying pan. When I arrived he deposited in my mess tin a large, thick slice of pork. One of his assistants was a butcher by trade and he had 'found' and slaughtered a porker. So that morning we ate. The meat was washed down with a mug of 'Sergeant-Major's'. This was a brew supposedly reserved for sergeant-majors, but which was greatly appreciated by the troops, especially in times of stress. It consisted of a very strong brew of tea to which had been added liberal quantities of evaporated milk and sugar. We would find it revolting nowadays, but then it satisfied and stimulated both body and mind.

I went into the office. I found that soon after I had left, the colonel had been summoned once more to Divisional HQ. On the way back he had briefed the battery commanders at one of their HQs. When he returned, the operation order over which I had laboured was cancelled and a new one was drafted, which Tug had typed. We were now to return to the Belgian front.

It transpired later that the operation which had been cancelled had been dreamed up by those self-esteemed armchair military strategists Churchill and Reynaud, the French premier, in a total lack of appreciation of conditions on the ground. For one thing, Churchill is said to have told General Gort to commit eight divisions to the attack without saying where they were to come from. All the BEF were already in action, Gort's two reserve divisions being those which had carried out the aborted attack two days before. Had the operation been carried out, success was unlikely, partly because of the superior strength of the enemy forces, but chiefly because they had undisputed command of the air, with a massive number of bombers and an apparently limitless supply of ammunition.

Failure would have meant that the BEF and the French army in the north would have been completely cut off from the coast. As it was, the reason the attack was cancelled was that the French army in the south could not carry it out until the following day. Communications within the French army were chaotic and those between the French and the British commanders even worse. General Gort failed to attend a meeting with the French supreme commander, General Weygand, because he did not receive notification of it until the following day! At the same time the Belgian army was crumbling in the face of the German onslaught. It was on this day that it was decided that the evacuation of the BEF should be attempted from the only available port, Dunkirk.

So General Gort switched his two reserve divisions, the 5th and the 50th, to the Belgian front. They were to be known as Frankforce, under the command of General Franklin of the 5th. The Belgian army was to be responsible for the sector from our left flank to the coast. The French were mostly to be responsible for the western front. We moved off quite soon. Our route took us round the northern outskirts of Armentières. It had been destroyed. Buildings were a mass of rubble and numerous fires were burning. I wondered what had become of the two elderly sisters with whom I had lodged, and the friendly bank clerk and his wife, who had entertained us so generously. The weasel words 'collateral damage' had not then been coined, but the Germans knew all about softening up their enemy, regardless of civilian casualties, before committing their land forces.

We passed through Nieppe and crossed the frontier, for the third time in a week, this time at Le Seau. As we went through Neuve-Église and Kemmel we found the urban areas had all been bombed. The open countryside, bathed in sunlight, remained peaceful as we trundled on our way towards Vlamertinghe, our destination. Soon after passing over the brow of a hill, however, there appeared a square of shell bursts, each about fifty yards from the road. They were obviously ranging shots from gunners who really knew their stuff. The next salvo would undoubtedly land on the road itself. The office truck was the third in line. By the time the 2 i/c had got out of his truck to wave an arm in a circular motion above his head, the drivers of all the vehicles which had reached the downward slope of the hill were executing smart three-point turns. The 2 i/c led us along a different road, through Dickebushe.

The regimental command post was set up in an attractive, well-maintained farmhouse. The batteries were deployed quite near and the guns were soon in action. The enemy, advancing rapidly, had not yet taken Ypres and targets were engaged beyond the town.

News arrived that the Belgian army had capitulated. The twenty-mile gap from our left flank to the coast was being filled by a British division. 'Fine', said the adjutant. 'We only need the French to pack it in and we'll know exactly where we stand!' It was only weeks before his gloomy prognostication came true. He went on to grumble: 'The British Army has never been taught to retreat. In all the exercises I have taken part in over the years retreat was never contemplated. The attack always succeeded'.

After my first rush of work on the artillery board had subsided, I walked through the back of the house to get a breath of air outside. I found something which I had seen described but never seen for myself. The farmhouse occupied one side of a rectangle, with outbuildings along each of the shorter sides. On the side opposite the house was a large barn. There was a wide concrete path all round and in the middle was a midden. This was full of straw cleared out of the cowshed, rotting fruit and vegetables and stank to high heaven. In it were a number of pigs, filthy dirty, rooting happily in all the muck. One of our drivers was Busty Cash, a lovely man. He was large, with a round, rosy, rustic face and an accent which I took to be Lincolnshire. He was entranced by the sight and, echoing a phrase popular in the army, said over and over again 'Ee! Pigs in shit! I never thought I would see it. Happy as pigs in bloody shit!'

A number of heavy bombers appeared, flying very low. The direction in which they were flying would take them to the left of us. As we watched each plane in turn released a stick of bombs. They fell, evenly spaced, in a graceful arc towards the ground. Once more Busty was moved to comment. 'Shelling peas!', he said, 'Just like shelling bloody peas!' We thought the target was probably Vlamertinghe and heard later that one bomb had fallen in the churchyard, with macabre effect.

We remained in action until nightfall when, under the cover of darkness, we were instructed to move. We went along country lanes, crossing the Ypres–Poperinghe road at a point midway between those towns, as a signpost told us. We passed some wooded land on our left beyond which we saw a column of flame and smoke which may have come from a crashed plane. We eventually arrived in our new position not far from Vlamertinghe, where gun pits and slit trenches had to be dug and the command post made ready for us to go into action at first light.

8

Tuesday 28 May 1940

That became the pattern of operations for the next few days. The guns were in action during the long hours of daylight. (It was approaching midsummer.) When darkness fell, the regiment left its positions, travelled a few miles north and set up its new positions before dawn. There was little time for anyone to sleep.

When we got to our new position, it was reported that 365 Battery had left a gun behind. The colonel sent for the gun position officer concerned and demanded an explanation. He was not satisfied with the excuses offered and ordered the officer to send back the No 1 and his men to collect the gun. 'You are not to go yourself', he added. Soon after he had gone intelligence came in that the Germans had advanced and that the route over which we had come was now behind the enemy FDLs (forward defended localities). Before the night was out, the troop commander returned to RHQ to report that the gun had been recovered. 'Which way did they come?', asked the colonel. 'The same way that we had all come earlier', said the officer. Somehow they had gone to the previous position and towed the gun back, without hindrance, behind the enemy lines. 'You went yourself, didn't you?', asked the colonel shrewdly. The officer admitted that he had. 'Hmm', was all the Colonel said. I presumed he was deferring comment until Tug and I were not present.

The withdrawal of the BEF through a gap only fifteen miles wide could be achieved only by the exercise of strict discipline. The few roads leading north already carried crowds of civilian refugees. Orders were given that all units withdrawn from action were to destroy all their equipment and vehicles and proceed on foot to the coast. Only units still in action could still drive. This involved a march for some units of up to fifty-five miles.

11 The Menin Gate at Ypres.

An officer from one of the batteries reported that he had seen a heavy anti-aircraft battery about to set out, having blown up their guns. I found it difficult to believe this. God knew, we needed their protection. One could only hope that those in authority had not lost their marbles.

The town of Ypres, through which the Germans had now advanced, was still well within our field of fire. A call came in over the field telephone from one of the battery commanders who wished to speak to the colonel. The latter picked up the phone and listened. 'Of course you fire', he said. 'Those whose names are inscribed on the memorial would not wish you to do otherwise'. 'We've been asked to engage machine gunners who are just in front of the Menin Gate. I hope we don't do too much damage', he remarked, after he put the phone down. I visited Ypres years afterwards and could see no scars on that side of the memorial.

I realised that I had not written home since we were at Lihus, over a fortnight before. Now that our precarious situation had been revealed at home, I thought I had better let them know I was all right. The letter, which I have still, illustrates the limitations imposed by the censorship rules to which we were subject. It reads as follows:

901457 L/Bdr Wild, RW   92nd Field Regiment, RA,
                                                    B.E.F.
                                              27 May 1940

Dear All,

There isn't any news to give, but I expect you would like a line to let you know that everything is O.K. and I am perfectly fit and enjoying the lovely summer weather.

I haven't heard from home lately, for the simple reason that the Post Office seems to have lost us again. I suppose there will be a stack for us when the mail does catch up with us.

Well, as I haven't any letters to answer, I'm left with nothing more that I can write about, so will simply say 'au revoir' and love to all.

We suddenly got busy again and I put my letter into my writing case.

That night, we moved a few miles north again, to the town of Oostaleteran, with the batteries between there and Westaleteren. The regimental command post was set up in a small house on the main Ypres–Nieuwpoort road. The occupants, a middle-aged couple, were about to leave. They were in a bad temper. Now that Belgium had capitulated they, and many of their compatriots, resented our presence. If we cleared off, the Germans would occupy their country, but it would not be devastated any more, they hoped.

They were taking food with them, including some large, flat loaves. Not having tasted bread for over a fortnight, Tug and I asked them to sell us one. They refused at first and then demanded an exorbitant price from which they would not budge. It took nearly all our francs, but we were hungry and paid them.

9

Wednesday 29 May 1940

As soon as we had set up the office, Tug and I cut slices of the bread. It was hard and dry. We had been done, but it was no worse than the ration biscuits and it was food of a sort. 'Hold on', said Tug. 'I'm going to have a look around', and dived out of the room. He returned with a small slab of butter, which was white and unsalted, and a small bowl of eggs. We appropriated them with glee. We felt we had paid for them.

Along the road in front of our house there was a continuous stream of troops trudging towards the coast. They walked in perfect order in squads of seven or eight men on alternate sides of the road, with a space of about fifty yards between squads. We also saw the occasional Belgian soldier. Each one, as I remember, was pushing a bicycle with his belongings piled on it and was wearing plimsolls. We heard that the next main road to the west, from Poperinghe to Dunkirk, was crowded with a disorganised mass of refugees and troops, as well as units trying to maintain some sort of order.

We had a new MO. He was a quiet, openly religious young man in contrast to the chaplain, who ran the rugby side and was, it seems, the one who organised social activities, sweepstakes etc. in the officers' mess. The MO had been sitting outside in the sunshine and came into the office tossing a piece of metal from one gloved hand to the other. It landed on my metal table with a dunk. 'Don't touch it. It's hot,' he said. It was a beautifully engineered shiny steel segment of a shrapnel shell. We had not heard a shell burst from indoors, so we concluded that it must have travelled a long way before it just missed him. He decided to stay under cover in future.

The adjutant went on a mission to the battery command posts on a motorcycle. He returned limping, having fallen off the

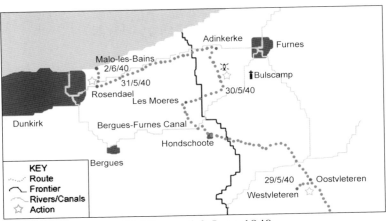

12 Action between 29 May and 2 June 1940.

machine. 'You're determined to get an honourable wound, aren't you, Charles', remarked the colonel. The adjutant just grunted. I do not think he appreciated the comment.

A truck arrived from the Army Post Office to collect mail — the first for several days. I remembered the letter, which I had written two days before so I scribbled on the bottom of it in pencil, 'Nothing to add. Everything O.K.' Lieut. Marsh censored it for me and I popped it into the bag. Goodness knows how, but it was eventually delivered.

We moved again that night, but had not gone far before we halted in a small town. The vehicles were parked and half a dozen of us were told to bivouac on the lawn in front of a house. As there were reliable reports that German parachutists were about we were instructed to take turns on guard. For this purpose we were given one rifle between us. My turn was to come at 3 a.m.

10

Thursday 30 May 1940

It was not very comfortable under the hedge where I was lying, but I managed to doze off and when my predecessor on guard woke me I was in a deep sleep. 'It's three o'clock', he said, handing me the rifle. 'There's one up the spout and the safety catch is on'. I had never done guard duty before. I decided that if there were parachutists about it would be silly to present myself as a target by standing in the open. I stood under the high hedge between the lawn and the road, near the gate.

It was fairly dark and very quiet I was still sleepy and, to stop myself from dozing off on my feet I tried to concentrate on thinking about specific things, but that did not work very well. After what seemed to be an age, I looked at my watch—it was ten past three. Another fifty minutes to go! I was brooding about this fact when I heard footsteps coming along the road. As they got louder I hoped they would go on past. At the gate they stopped and as it swung open I thrust my rifle into the midriff of the figure which entered, my thumb on the safety catch and my finger on the trigger. If it was an enemy I had no intention of missing. 'Halt! Who goes there?' I yelled. 'Hell, Wild', said one of our officers. 'You bloody nearly gave me a heart attack. Wake up the others and all of you get along to where the trucks are parked straight away'.

It was daylight when we set off. We crossed the border into France and came into Hondschoote from the east. The waves of Stukas started early and there were other formations too—Heinkels, Dorniers and Messerschmitt fighters, all heading towards Dunkirk. In Hondschoote we met roads coming from the south and these were full of traffic of every description—British and French troops, many with trucks, Bren gun carriers etc., and civilians with the usual assortment of cars, lorries, prams and bicycles. The troops on foot were in good order, but I wondered why so many units which were no longer fighting had retained their vehicles. Just beyond the town the main road onto which all the traffic had converged crossed the Bergues–Furnes canal, which was the final defence line for Dunkirk. Here there was a tremendous bottleneck. Military police would not allow any troops to take their vehicles across unless, like us, they were entitled to do so. They all had to be destroyed, together with the equipment they were carrying. The whole area was littered with destroyed equipment.

Once we had crossed the canal we turned east, away from the crowded road, and entered Belgium once more. The countryside was quite different from the other side of the canal. It was very flat, mostly grassland, and was intersected by canals and narrow lanes all at right-angles to each other. The column halted as we travelled alongside one of these canals. There was a strip of grass between the road and the canal on one side and on the other a grass field. A flotilla of Stukas was flying overhead when someone shouted 'Look out'. We looked up and saw that three of the planes had peeled off the formation and were wheeling to come down in our direction. We scattered. I ran several paces towards the canal and threw myself to the ground, pressing down to present as small a target as possible to any bombs which might fall. There were no bombs, but an almost indescribable noise as the three Stukas dived together. To the scream of their engines were added the piercing sound of their sirens and the chatter of their machine-guns.

One's imagination is no friend in such circumstances. I saw in my mind's eye the row of bullet holes in the wall at Givenchy and seemed to feel a similar stream of bullets running up my spine. Then the planes had gone. We picked ourselves up. The planes had flown abreast, the one in the centre firing at the vehicles and the others at the men on each side of the road. We found to our relief that, scattered as we were, no-one had been hit. Similarly, the vehicles had been too far apart to present sufficiently good targets.

A little later on we saw a British plane—our first since the campaign began. It was a Hercules, which had crash-landed. It did not seem badly damaged and we hoped the pilot had got out safely.

Our new position was about three miles south of Adinkerke. The hamlet of Moeres was just to our rear. The farm which the colonel had selected for the regimental command post was a remarkable place. We came to it from the rear. The farmhouse was snowy white and what would normally be the midden had been grassed over and made into an enormous aviary as high as the house itself. In this aviary white doves fluttered and on the ground were bantams and rabbits, most of them white. To the left of the aviary there was a range of well-kept outbuildings which were allocated to the Royal Corps of Signals detachment. Opposite the house were a number of barns in which our vehicles were hidden The other (north) side of the quadrangle was open. In front of the house there was a small flower garden and shrubbery, an unusual feature in a working farm, especially in this area.

The house had a cellar which was dean, dry and uncluttered and admirably suited for our purpose, but it had no light. All we had were a few torches. Tug and I went prospecting through the house and found two big oil lamps. They had large rose-coloured glass bowls, full of oil, and when lit they gave an excellent light.

When we had brought in our equipment I went out to the signals office. To my surprise I saw approaching an attractive girl about seventeen years old with a younger boy. They were well dressed and evidently came from this unusual farm. 'Why are you here?' I asked. 'Is it dangerous?' she asked. The 365 Battery command post was nearby and the guns of one of its troops had actually been mounted in the garden. I thought of the Stork, circling as usual above. 'It is very dangerous', I said. 'The Germans are less than two kilometres away'. She then said that there were two lamps, which she would like to take away. This put me into a quandary. We really needed the light. I told her so, but asked if she would be satisfied with one. I said we would be careful with the other and hoped it would still be here, intact, when, they were able to return. She agreed at once, so I went into the cellar to get the lamp. When I returned, I found her in the kitchen. I handed the lamp over and she gave me a jar. 'For you', she said. I thanked her and said she and her brother must go as quickly as possible. When we went outside, she glanced towards the garden and saw one of the guns in the shrubbery. She burst into tears. I watched them until they were out of sight to make sure they really had gone. We found that the jar she had given me contained pickled plums. Tug and I shared them. They went down well with ration biscuits.

In the centre of the sector allotted to the regiment there was a white windmill on each side of which the batteries were deployed. As the windmill was the only possible position for an elevated observation post in this flat countryside, the colonel ordered that it should be used by each battery in turn. Opposite this position and a little to the right, at a distance of 4,000 yards, was the parish church of Bulscamp. Its tower was the only elevated observation post for the Germans. It was decided that an effort should be made to render it untenable, so fire was opened up on it. Hits were positively registered, bits of masonry having been seen to fall, and it was claimed that the belfry had been destroyed. If this was true it would be a setback for the German artillery, but they still had the Stork!

Firing was almost continuous, with our infantry frequently calling for specific targets to be engaged. The brigade which we were supporting consisted of three battalions of the Durham Light Infantry. Our Signals detachment came, as I have mentioned, from Bedford. A message came in from the Signals office: 'ENGAGE FRENCH MOTORS AT ... ' and it gave the coordinates. I glanced at the message and told the signalman to wait. The colonel read it and said, as I expected, 'Have it checked'. A few minutes later the message came back 'ENGAGE TRENCH MORTARS AT ... .' It was like a deadly game of Chinese whispers.

A message was received from the Commander-in-Chief saying that he had received a telegram from the King which was to be passed on to all troops. It read as follows:

All your countrymen have been following with pride and admiration the courageous resistance of the British Expeditionary Force during the continuous fighting of the last fortnight. Placed by circumstances outside their control in a position of extreme difficulty they are displaying a gallantry that has never been surpassed in the annals of the British Army. The hearts of every one of us at home are with you and your magnificent troops in this hour of peril.

Then followed the C-in-C's reply:

The Commander-in-Chief, with humble duty, begs leave on behalf of all ranks in the British Expeditionary Force to thank your Majesty for your message. May I assure your Majesty that the Army is doing all in its power to live up to its proud traditions and is immensely encouraged at this critical moment by the words of your Majesty's telegram.

The King's message confirmed that our position was serious enough for those in authority at home to be worried. We had no idea how the evacuation was proceeding, simply that as we moved nearer the coast, we moved closer to the possibility of our getting back to England.

According to what an officer in one of the batteries wrote later, the officers of his battery took the messages very seriously, especially the phrases 'hour of peril' and 'critical moment'. They thought that from this position we might have to march on foot to Dunkirk. They decided to do so in their best clothes and to get rid of as much kit as possible so as to travel light. He recounts how, with his batman, he sorted his kit into two piles — a little pile of what he could take and a big pile of what he could not. He put on a clean shirt and another went into his pack with clean pants, vest, towel, pyjamas, shaving kit and toothbrush. He decided to wear his *best* tunic and his *best* breeches, puttees and boots. He told his batman to put all the rest into the suitcase and get as far as he could to England with it all. If he had to jettison anything, the camp bed was to go first, then the suitcase, then the pack. The orders we had received three weeks before to put all our spare kit into our kit-bags to be sent home apparently did not apply to officers. His *best* service dress indeed!

In their defence, as they had the kit still with them, it was understandable that the officers should array themselves in their finery. They knew perfectly well that once the rearguard fell back towards the beaches, the enemy might attack in force, overwhelm us and make escape impossible. Those who survived would inevitably be captured. Whatever happened they intended to face it with dignity and aplomb. They were good soldiers who had proved themselves in battle to be both competent and courageous, so a touch of bravado could perhaps be forgiven.

Their mess cook had been instructed to use his imagination in producing that evening's meal. He produced a candle-lit dinner with an array of red and white wines. The menu was tomato soup, four roast chickens, potatoes, peas, fruit salad, sardines on toast as a savoury, cheese and coffee. Half rations were acceptable no doubt if the mess had a truckful of goodies with which to supplement them and some mess servants who were good scroungers!

We had found a wireless set in the house and that evening we gathered round it to listen to the nine o'clock news on the BBC Home Service. The first item was to the effect that the RAF had continued to give massive support to the BEF as it withdrew through Dunkirk and claimed the destruction of great numbers, running into three figures, of enemy planes. 'The lying bastards', expostulated one of the officers. We had still not seen one RAF plane in the air to tackle the massive formations of enemy bombers. 'It's a pity they can't spare one fighter to shoot down that bloody spotter plane', said another, referring to the ever-present Stork. It transpired later that where the RAF had engaged with the enemy was over the Dunkirk beaches. The claims of enemy 'kills' were vastly exaggerated and official figures later showed that the RAF had lost at least as many planes as the Germans. The RAF, however, gave no support to the rearguard which was still fighting to hold the enemy back to make evacuation possible.

For some days previously, when we were in action all day and moving all night, Tug and I had taken turns, when only one was required to be on duty, to lie down under our table in an attempt to get some sleep. We chose this position because space was always limited in the command post and to lie anywhere else would mean our getting under someone's feet. Tug was asleep when the colonel and adjutant returned from a meeting at Infantry Brigade HQ and picked up Lieut. Marsh on the way in. The infantry had been pushed back during the afternoon and proposed to counter-attack at dawn under cover of an artillery barrage. The officers set about working out the details, which they transferred to the artillery board. It was to be a massive operation, involving the whole of the regiment. It was complicated in that at the halfway stage it was to change direction about 45 degrees to the left. When their work was completed it was my job to trace copies. Accuracy was essential as the infantry had to know the exact timing and extent of each 'lift'. I was thankful for the good light from the lamp, which I had been able to keep. I had to produce copy after copy, one for each of the two batteries and for each of the six troops and copies for the infantry. When the last of the copies had been despatched, well after midnight, I woke Tug and took his place under the table. It had been a long day, starting as it did when I went on guard duty at 3 a.m.

11

Friday 31 May 1940

When I woke up, I said to Tug 'I didn't hear the barrage'. He replied, 'That's because there wasn't one. The DLI had attacked in the dark, before the barrage was due, taken Jerry by surprise and retaken the ground they had lost'. Tug, a Geordie himself, was immensely proud of the Durham Light Infantry, as was I, having been born in County Durham. So for the second time I had worked long and hard into the night in preparation for an operation which was called off.

It was yet another lovely day. The bombers had started passing over us on their way to Dunkirk soon after it was light and the Stork was circling overhead as usual. What was alarming, however, was that a manned observation balloon had appeared in the direction of Furnes. It was beyond the range of any fire which our troops were able to bring to bear on it. We could imagine a smug German officer sitting there, able to watch our every move through his binoculars. Oh for a fighter plane to shoot him down!

The morning was passing in what had become routine. One or other of the troops would open fire on a target requested by the infantry. Then there was a report that enemy troops were moving up in force to the right of our sector, presumably in preparation for an attack. The colonel ordered the whole regiment to open rapid fire on the target area with, the observation officer reported, success, in that the attack seemed to have been called off.

I was taking a message to the Signals office for transmission when I met a signalman coming the other way. We exchanged the messages we were carrying and were having a chat, thankful for a spell in the open air, when a shell whistled overhead and exploded in the field beyond the barns. Almost instantaneously another went off some fifty yards in front of the farmhouse.

'They could have been ranging shots', I said. 'We'd better get under cover.'

I had barely got back into the cellar when there was a crash overhead and a deafening explosion. This was followed by other shell bursts, some nearby and others farther away. The colonel said 'This is heavy stuff, 5.9 at least'. The Germans had evidently brought up their medium artillery and we were receiving their attention. The house above us was hit again, then again. Rubble tumbled down on to the floor above us. Fortunately, it did not give way, otherwise we would have been buried. The colonel picked up the field telephone, but the Signals sergeant who answered told him that all the lines had been cut. After what seemed to be an eternity but which was probably not more than fifteen minutes, the firing ceased and the colonel and adjutant rushed out to see what had happened.

I went soon after, to see if Signals had any information. When I opened the cellar door, I stepped out, not into the hallway, which ran from back to front of the house, but into the open air. To the front, the shrubbery had disappeared and we looked straight across the open fields to the buildings, which we knew to be beyond the enemy's front fine. I felt terribly vulnerable — imagination again, because common sense told me that I was out of sniper range, but I hated the idea that I could be seen. To the back, the building occupied by the Signals section was unscathed, but all the wire netting to the aviary had vanished. The grass was untouched, but the only living thing visible was a white rabbit, sitting up on its haunches. Several of the barns, in which our vehicles had been hidden, had been destroyed.

From beyond the barns came distressing and unexpected sounds. Unknown to us, a French horse-drawn munitions train had drawn into the field just before the bombardment started. When the shells began to fall, all the men had fled leaving the horses still harnessed to the wagons. The sounds I heard were the neighing of terrified animals, mingled with the screams of those, which had been wounded. Then there were rifle shots. I have said that some of our drivers were former drivers RA, trained horsemen, and they had set about freeing the horses from their harness and putting the injured ones out of their misery.

I returned to the cellar. News soon began to come in as to what had happened, and it was bad. Every part of the regiment had been bombarded simultaneously. This I recognised from my training at Larkhill was counter-battery work of the highest order. Had only one battery been targeted, the other could have opened up in defence. As it was, thanks to the balloon and the Stork, the enemy had been able to pinpoint not only our gun positions but also our command posts and wagon lines and must have used an entire regiment of medium guns in an endeavour to wipe us out. We first heard that a shell had exploded at the entrance to 365 Battery command post, killing the battery commander and four of his men. Guns had been hit in the troop nearby and more men killed. The other battery reported more fatalities and the loss of guns.

It was obvious that our position was untenable and it came as no surprise, and some relief, to receive orders to move. As our office truck was now out of action, Tug and I were told to travel in Z2, the 2 i/c's 8 cwt, as he travelled with the colonel. We took our metal box, with its precious documents, message pads etc., and everything else we could carry and climbed aboard. We had not gone far and were still on the farm, when the engine petered out. We found that the petrol tank had been pierced by shell splinters. Fortunately, the reserve tank was intact but when the driver pressed the starter button the engine refused to start. 'I expect the auto-vac's dry', said the driver. This was Greek to me. He took off the top of this bit of the works and found that it had been drained. He said it would have to be primed, but he had no spare petrol can. We therefore dipped a handkerchief into the fuel tank and squeezed it out into the auto-vac until it was full, a very slow job. The driver replaced the top, pressed the, starter button and Lo! the engine fired—it was the first bit of luck that day.

We joined the regimental convoy on the lane leading north to Adinkerke. We reached the main road and turned towards Dunkirk. We crossed the border into France once more and came to the outskirts of the district of Rosendaal, about four miles from the centre of Dunkirk. Here we occupied a brick-field, which consisted of long stacks of bricks about eight feet high and eight feet wide. The vehicles were parked between the rows and, because there were no buildings, our office was established in a similar position. Tug and I started to dig a slit trench. Because the soil was pure sand it was easy, but we came to the water table only two feet down, so to dig further would be useless.

We learned that we were to be one of four Field Artillery regiments to man the eastern and southern sectors of the last line of defence. The French were still responsible for the western sector. On our left was the 18th Field Regiment and on our right the 27th, both of them regular units. I do not remember which was the fourth regiment. Our remaining twelve guns were deployed near the village of Leffrinckoucke. Emplacement could not be carried out in the normal way because of the high water table. Instead, sandbag walls had to be built up round the guns.

In that flat, open country with no available cover and no slit trenches, the gunners felt, and were, very vulnerable. They were not best pleased, therefore, when one of the troop commanders in 368 Battery started cavorting up and down on a white horse he had found. Suddenly there was a loud noise overhead like the rushing of an express train. The officer realised what it was. He rose in his stirrups and raised an arm. 'Hurrah boys', he declaimed, 'the Navy's here'. The men were not so gung-ho as some of their officers and were in no mood for such emotional gestures. There was an embarrassed silence, broken by a querulous cockney voice. 'Wot we s'posed to do then, break out in bleedin' boils?'

The sound of the Navy's heavy guns, which fired only intermittently, was in marked contrast to that of a French battery of 75 mm guns which, unknown to us had taken up position in the field just behind us. These guns have a very flat trajectory and the shells passed low over our heads with the sound like the crack of a whip.

For the first time we saw the RAF in action. The German bombers comprised not only Stukas but Heinkels and Dorniers too. Above them flew Messerschmitt fighters. The RAF Spitfires had the disadvantage of having to fly from their bases in

England, so they could spend only twenty minutes in combat. They were also seriously short of men and planes. In consequence, the Germans had intervals during which they were unmolested. When the RAF did arrive, they had to cope with the Messerschmitts before they could get at the bombers. They were, however, able to shoot some down. The air battles were farther away than I had expected as the nearest beach was only about a mile away as the crow flies. I learned later that this was because the bombers were now concentrating on the ships lying offshore and trying to reach the harbour, leaving the men on the beaches and the small boats to the tender mercies of the artillery.

This was obviously to be our last position and orders were received for our vehicles to be destroyed. This was both a heart-rending and ear-shattering operation. The engines were started and then the radiators and oil sumps allowed to drain. As the engines got hotter and hotter the noise became deafening until at last they seized up. Then tyres, seats and canvas coverings were slashed, lamps and glass smashed, electrical parts ripped out and everything possible done to leave nothing which would be of use to the enemy.

As darkness fell, the air raids ceased, but the enemy artillery continued to shell the beaches and the ships lying offshore. Operation Dynamo was supposed to have ended in the early hours of this morning but, fortunately for us, the Navy was determined to carry on whilst there were men to be evacuated and they could get the ships there to get them.

12

Saturday 1 June 1940

The short night passed. In the morning orders were received for all married men who could be spared to proceed to the coast. Tug protested, but he had a wife and small child and there was little for us to do anyway, so off he trudged with the rest. For the first time rumours filtered through to us as to what was happening. There was talk of ships being sunk, including paddle steamers like the *Gracie Fields* and the *Crested Eagle*, of the east mole being breached and of men waiting for days in the dunes. At midday all the remaining men not needed to man the guns were sent. There remained with me in RHQ only the colonel and adjutant, the colonel's driver and his batman, an old soldier who refused to leave him. He had no real reason to stay, because the colonel no longer had any kit for him to look after, since it had been in an upper room of the farmhouse and so completely destroyed. The batman's son, the butcher who had provided for us the pork breakfast, would not leave his father. The colonel ordered the Signals section to leave us two field telephones, each connected to a battery command post, and to destroy their exchange and the rest of their equipment. Then they all went too.

For the first time for what seemed an eternity I had nothing to do but man the field telephones, which did not ring often as the colonel spent most of the time at one or other of the batteries. The hours of the afternoon and evening passed slowly. I had nothing to do but think, apart from watching the aerial combat. The enemy bombers came over but were disturbed from time to time as fighters arrived from England. The aircraft started tumbling from the sky. I knew the bombers were German but aircraft recognition was not my strong point and I did not know whose fighters were shot down. Official figures published later showed that 29 enemy aircraft had been destroyed, whilst the

RAF lost 31.

During the tranquil intervals I gazed up into the cloudless blue sky in the direction of the Channel and England. For the first time in what seemed to be an age I was able to think about personal matters. I thought of what I wanted to do most in the world—to be married to Anne, to set up home, raise a family. I tried to picture it, but no picture presented itself. My thoughts turned to County Hall, speculating how my career would develop. Again, I got nowhere. I wondered if this was a sign that the days I visualised were not to be. I thought that perhaps I was doomed to be a prisoner of war, or killed, but here again my imagination failed to function. It was as though I had been reading a biography of myself, come to the end of Part I and then found that all the subsequent pages were blank, or like an actor who, having come to the end of the first act of a play, finds that he has no idea what happens to his character in the rest of it. I seemed to have reached a full stop, or at least a colon. I found the experience strange, but not alarming. I was neither excited nor afraid. Looking back, I have come to the conclusion that I had become so absorbed into the military machine, by a process intensified under battle conditions, that I would automatically do whatever I was ordered to do. Senior NCOs were fond of telling us that we were not paid to think but 'to do as we were bloody well told'. My mind had apparently absorbed this completely.

One of the battery commanders reported that the enemy had advanced down the coast. This was in the 18th Field Regiment's sector, but we had been ordered to stand by in reserve. The colonel then heard that because of this advance the beaches at La Panne and Bray-Dunes were no longer to be used, leaving only that at Malo-les-Bains.

We were supposed to remain in action until midnight. This was brought forward to 11.00 p.m. when preparation for the destruction of the guns was to be commenced. This was expected to be completed by 11.30. A suggestion was made that our few remaining rounds of ammunition should be fired off at random, but the colonel ruled this out, stating that to do so would be likely to provoke the enemy into retaliation to no good purpose. As it was nearly midsummer, darkness came very late. It did not seem very long after it fell before the final steps were being taken by the gunners. Spare shells were dumped into the nearby canal. Cordite was emptied from the cartridge cases to be burnt immediately before the gunners left. Each gun was loaded and another shell inserted into the barrel face down. The No. 1 attached a very long lanyard to the trigger. At 11.30 both Battery Commanders reported they were ready. The colonel told me to dismantle the phones. I took each to pieces and threw the component parts in different directions as far as I could.

We listened, then there was a rending crack as the first gun was destroyed, then another. We knew that the explosion as the shells met would rip the barrel like the peel of a banana and damage the breech block irreparably. It was a heart-wrenching sound. The colonel's face was grim but, as ever, composed. 'We may as well ride to the beach', he said. 'There won't be any traffic'. So we all piled into his Humber. I took my metal box with me. 'Get those papers back to England, Wild, won't you?', said the adjutant. He did not add 'if you can'. We drove to the main road and turned towards the town. The canal on our right was between us and the coast but after a couple of miles there was a turning to the right which crossed it. We went along this until we came to the road running above the dunes at the eastern end of Malo-les-Bains. We set about destroying the car.

13

Sunday 2 June 1940

It was now past midnight. An officer carrying a clipboard came up to us. 'What unit are you from, sir?' he asked the colonel. The colonel told him and added 'This officer and I are going to wait for the rest of my regiment. The men are to carry on'. The beach marshal, for such he was, told us to get down to the beach and to walk towards the harbour until we met another marshal. We picked our way across the dunes down on to the beach and across the soft dry sand until we found some from which the sea had receded—leaving it firm.

It was a wonderful, balmy night. Looking out to sea, a thousand stars shone brightly. The sea was very calm and the tide reached the shallow shore in tiny wavelets, which broke into a line of phosphorescence, a phenomenon I had never seen before. Our footprints in the damp sand also shone with phosphorescence. Even the shrapnel as its fragments flew through the air glowed red. Fortunately, the enemy gunners had a very wide target, from the dunes to the ships lying offshore, and none of the bursts came near enough to menace us.

If the prospect looking seawards was pleasing, in the other direction there was convincing proof that man is indeed vile. Dozens of fires raged in the town, silhouetting the skeletons of buildings, which had been destroyed by shell or bomb. Looking straight ahead the breakwater stretching out into the deep water stood out black against an even more fiery background. The whole of the western sky was a mass of flame, suggesting that at least one fuel depot in the dock area was ablaze. Over all there were no stars to be seen for the whole area was covered with a massive pall of smoke on which the flames below were reflected.

We trudged towards the breakwater, which was about a mile away. We could see that we would not be embarking from it because not far from the landward end there was a gap. My friend Bob Paxton told me later that he had been at the seaward end, with a crowd of others, when the gap had been blasted and they had had to wait, in that horribly exposed situation, for hours, unable to get ashore, with the ships being shelled and bombed as they tried to get to the pier to take them off. We seemed to be getting no nearer and my box felt heavier and heavier. Then at last we came upon another beach marshal. He told us to join a small double queue of men near the water's edge. We had not been there long before three naval rowing boats appeared, one with an outboard engine towing the other two. All were full before our turn came, but the petty officer in charge called out 'Stay there. We'll be back'.

It was not pleasant, standing in the water, so several of us clambered onto the back of a 15 cwt, which had been abandoned nearby. We waited for what seemed to be ages before we heard the welcome put-put of the outboard engine. We jumped down from the truck to find ourselves waist deep in water. We had forgotten the tide was coming in. I was near the prow of the leading boat. I handed up my box to a sailor but he said 'Sorry. No luggage, mate'. I told him that the box contained regimental papers, which I had been told to get home. He took the box, then leaned over and hauled me into the boat. All the boats filled rapidly and we set off into the darkness. As the boat I was in pulled the others seawards one of them turned over. 'Cast it off', said the petty officer. We started to protest at the men being left floundering in the water. 'They'll be all right', he said. 'It's shallow and we'll be back for them. We don't want to lose our boat, anyway'.

We could see little in the darkness but suddenly found ourselves alongside a naval ship, which loomed above us. It had a climbing net hanging over the side. The sailor who had helped me took my box and nipped up the net to hand it to another sailor on the deck. 'No luggage', said that worthy. It seemed to be some sort of mantra. My friendly sailor said 'It's all right. It's full of official papers'. The other took his word for it and accepted the box. Meanwhile, I was trying to climb the net but had not got far before I realised it was beyond me. I was fit but my greatcoat and uniform were heavy with seawater. I was hungry and physically exhausted. My sailor friend saw my predicament, grabbed me round the waist and hauled me up and onto the deck.

I retrieved my box and joined the other soldiers who were being shepherded down below. Further along the deck there was a commotion. We asked what it was but were simply told to get a move on. A little later we heard that the ship's medical officer had been killed by shrapnel. I had been so preoccupied with getting aboard the ship that I had not even noticed that it was being shelled.

As I approached the superstructure of the ship I saw on it a huge plaque bearing the battle honour 'The Glorious First of June'. How appropriate, I thought, though by now it was well into the second of June. To my lasting regret, I have never been able to recall the name of the vessel. I do not even know if it was a minesweeper or mine-layer.

On the ratings' messdeck we were seated on forms on each side of a long table. It was very warm, which was just as well in view of our soaked state. Sailors put before us large mugs of soup and hunks of bread. After a fortnight without bread, any bread would have been more than acceptable, but this bread was sheer luxury — soft, white and freshly baked. After we had eaten we settled down for a doze, but the sailors said they had been instructed to keep us awake. They now produced mugs of creamy cocoa, which went down extremely well. I will always feel admiration and gratitude for the sailors on that ship. Though, unlike us, they were clean and well fed, they had for days been under severe stress and constant danger but were still cheerful and helpful.

The ship's engines stopped and we went up on deck to find that it was broad daylight and we were in Dover harbour. We had only to cross the quay to board a train. This was one of what was then fairly new Southern Railway stock, with dining car type carriages and what were to us blissfully upholstered seats. The train moved off without delay but got only as far as Paddock

Wood when it stopped again, to be boarded by Guardsmen bearing our breakfast. This consisted of individual steak and kidney pies. When we got moving again we were surprised to see all along the line knots of people waving to us. As the train pulled into Tonbridge station, we saw that the platform was full of women and girls in bright summer dresses waving and calling their greetings. When the train stopped, they handed through the open windows tea and lemonade, sweets, cigarettes and cakes. They also produced postcards saying 'Home safely' which they invited us to address, when the Post Office would deliver them promptly and free of postage. Unfortunately, no one seems to have told the Post Office. Mine took a fortnight to get there. Just before the train drew out, bundles of Sunday newspapers arrived. The one I got was the *Sunday Express*. Across the front page was the banner headline:

Last Night's Ordeal of the Last Thin Line of Dunkirk

'Hell!' I said, 'Our people at home must be worried about us'. I had not heard a news broadcast since Thursday and had no idea that the Government had at long last revealed to the British public the dire situation in France.

After a similar greeting in Guildford station we finally arrived at Aldershot and were taken by truck to an emergency tented camp, which was being run by an officer cadet unit. After our particulars had been taken, we were each issued with blankets and a ground sheet and shown the tent we were to occupy.

The notepaper in my writing case, which I had carried in my haversack, was miraculously dry and I settled down to write a letter to Anne. Whilst writing it I fell asleep and was woken three hours later to get a meal. I went back to my tent feeling considerably refreshed and completed the letter. (Anne typed a copy of it, leaving out the more personal passages, and I have used it to refresh my memory of those last days in Belgium and France.) I took the letter to the office tent, hoping to find a post box. I was increasingly concerned to let Anne and my parents know that I was back in England, so I asked if I might use the phone. I was told that no personal calls were allowed—the line must be kept available for official calls. I was determined to get hold of a telephone somehow and decided to risk going outside the camp.

I was very scruffy. My uniform had by now dried on me but the effects of its immersion were all too obvious and I had long lost my forage cap and refused to don my steel helmet again. I knew the dress code was strictly enforced in the Aldershot district, but felt thoroughly bolshie. After all, I had only one stripe to lose. I went to the gate expecting to be stopped but the cadets manning it looked the other way and I went out to find a telephone box. There was no sign of one, nor indeed of a village. I walked along the lane, keeping my eye on the telephone wires till one branched off up the drive of a large house.

I rang the doorbell. A well-dressed middle-aged woman came to the door. I asked her if I might please use her phone. She obviously (and understandably) did not like the look of me. She said 'I'm sorry, but we do not allow soldiers to do that'. 'O.K.', I said, 'be like that', and turned away. After I had gone a few steps she called out, 'Are you one of the troops from Dunkirk?' When I said I was, she invited me in, took me into her drawing room and seated me in an armchair with the phone beside me. 'Carry on', she said and left the room. Neither my parents nor Anne's were on the phone, but I knew the number of the latters' neighbour. I got through and when Mrs Cooke answered I asked her if she would take a message to Anne. 'That's Ralph, isn't it?', she said. 'Hold on. I'll get her'. A minute or two later a breathless voice said 'Hello'. 'It's me', I said. There was a long silence. 'Are you still there?' I asked. 'Yes', was the reply, 'I'm just getting my breath back'. She wanted to know if I was all right, how I had got to England, when I would get some leave, etc. I said I was fit, but tired, that I had posted a long letter to her and that I should get some leave soon. Then there were more personal exchanges, which need not be recorded.

My hostess returned to the room bearing a tray of tea. I felt very out of place in my disreputable-looking state, with my heavy Army boots, sitting in that elegant drawing room, drinking tea out of real china cups. However, the welcome we had received since landing, from the Guards at Paddock Wood, the women at Tonbridge and Guildford, the cadets in the camp and now from this lady was heart-warming and I really felt that I was home again.

14

Monday 3 June 1940 and after

The next day we were moved from the reception camp to the assembly points of our respective formations. The 50th Division was encamped at Tatton Park, a large country estate near Knutsford in Cheshire. When I arrived I found the colonel and adjutant had already arrived. They must have been taken there direct from Dover, for they had only made the crossing that night. The up-to-date documents, especially the nominal rolls, which I had preserved in the metal box were invaluable when it came to checking off the men as they arrived. By Wednesday 5 June fifteen officers and 240 other ranks had rejoined the regiment. Our final figures showed that, out of about 660 all ranks, including attachments, we had lost about 60, including 16 killed. The regiment had been awarded two Military Crosses and three Military Medals.

The Adjutant sent for Tug and me. Since we arrived, I had not seen the sergeant artillery clerk and Tug had spotted him once. The adjutant said 'You will not see Sergeant ... any more. The colonel has agreed that you should both be made artillery clerks and promoted to bombardier. We consider you have proved yourselves in the field so an examination is unnecessary'. We thanked him but then, after looking at each other, told him that the regiment was entitled to only one artillery clerk. 'That's all right' said the adjutant airily. 'He should be a sergeant. I'll have two bombardiers instead'. Unfortunately, RA Records did not agree. A few weeks later an order arrived posting Tug to a Heavy Artillery regiment in Iceland(c). This was Army speak to avoid confusion with Ireland(r). Tug took it very well. All the adjutant said was 'I'll be sorry to lose you, Wilson. You'd better put up your third stripe, Wild'. So, six weeks after belatedly being paid for my first stripe, I now had three.

As I have mentioned, we had a wonderful reception from the public at large. Commentators in the press and on the wireless, including war correspondents, were generous in their praise for our efforts and their sentiments were echoed in American papers, which had their own correspondents. We soon had an indication that the attitude of the Government was completely different. A parade was called of all ranks of corporal or bombardier and above. The divisional commander, Major-General Martel, started by commending the troops under his command for their performance, especially as members of the rearguard, which had held the enemy advance on the Belgian side of the border, making evacuation of the main body of the BEF possible. He made special mention of the 92nd Field Regiment, RA, for its contribution and said it would soon be returning to the 5th Division.

He then said that he had been instructed to pass on verbal orders from the Government that all ranks were to be informed that severe disciplinary action would be taken against anyone who said anything in public critical of the RAF, however justified that might be in his own eyes. Apparently there had already been scuffles in pubs between members of the respective services and Churchill was thought to be scared of the effect on public morale if the misleading bulletins put out through the BBC and the newspapers were exposed.

We speculated as to how much leave we would get. We had had no embarkation leave before sailing to France and only one spell of seven days in the nine months since we were called up. We knew that the troops at home had been granted seven days leave every three months plus some weekend passes. And how about disembarkation leave? We were disgruntled, therefore, to receive passes for only seven days. When we had been paraded to be taken to the station, a sergeant-major collected all our passes from us and took them to the regimental office. When he brought them back, we were dismayed to find that the seven days had been reduced to two! The official reason was that, as battle-hardened troops we had to be available to meet an enemy invasion, which might be imminent. This was poppycock. There should by now be plenty of trained troops among those who had never left Britain. We had neither arms, equipment nor transport. Some of the replacements were still to be manufactured and would take weeks or months to be supplied. Our losses of men, which in the case of some units were grievous, had to be made up and the reinforcements trained and integrated, a process which could take some time. We were battle-hardened, certainly, but we were also battle-weary. It was likely that a number of men would have been traumatised by their experiences, some of them severely so. Nowadays, 'Counselling' would have been the answer. (Some of their relatives would demand it too!) In those days we were expected to 'pull ourselves together and get on with it'.

Churchill insisted that Dunkirk was not something to be celebrated. It was a defeat—the BEF had been 'kicked out of France'. He refused to authorise the striking of a Dunkirk star. (The brave defenders of Norway, Greece and Crete were treated in the same way.) Yet, later, a man or woman who landed in France long after D-Day and had never been near an actual battle zone, received the Europe Star. Churchill seemed to ignore the BEF's shortages and inadequacies of equipment, the paucities of their reserves, the lack of communication with the French generals who were supposed to be in overall command, and the severing of the impossibly long lines of communication when the German Panzers broke through the French defences and reached the Channel coast. Above all, he ignored the fact that the Luftwaffe was free to bomb and strafe us and keep us under continuous surveillance with impunity. In practice, the factors which had led the King, in his telegram to us, to say that the BEF had been 'placed by circumstances outside their control in a position of extreme difficulty' were not taken into consideration.

This implied denigration of the Army, as we saw it, was made worse by praise for the RAF for what, in fact, it did not do in the sense conveyed to the public. This caused unnecessary friction between the soldiers and the 'Brylcream Boys', as they contemptuously called them. This was not the fault of the RAF. It lost all its aircraft stationed in France soon after the Germans

13 The author's Albert Medal (left) and a medal awarded by the town of Dunkirk.

invaded. It was desperately short of men and aircraft to defend the homeland. Like the Army it was short of men and equipment owing to the failure of the Baldwin Government to respond to Churchill's repeated calls for rearmament in view of the Nazi government's increasingly belligerent policies. During the campaign Bomber Command attacked the German lines of communication, something which we, of course, could not see. Fighter Command fought courageously above the beaches of Dunkirk, suffering grievous losses. It could not afford to lose these machines, still less the airmen who manned them. The Army's rearguard, however, was left without cover.

Winston Churchill's rhetoric at this time was obviously designed to boost the morale of the British public. No doubt it had this effect and it certainly established him as a war hero and world statesman. My personal opinion, however, is that 'economy with the truth' was neither justified nor necessary. I had seen the ordinary British soldier in situations where disaster seemed inevitable, but it did not prevent him carrying on with his particular job. The attitude of the British public in general would have been the same. 'Spin' had not been invented in those days, but Churchill was a master of the art in comparison with whom the present practitioners are amateurs. The squaddy's inelegant term for it is 'bullshit', and he looks down on it in disdain. Looking back, it is my opinion that it was at this time that the first pebbles were dislodged which developed into the avalanche that swept Churchill from power at the 1945 general election.

Operation Dynamo was a magnificent achievement by the Royal Navy and the civilian volunteers without whom even the Navy could not have coped. It was carried out with the utmost skill, courage and self-sacrifice. Of a total of 693 ships of all kinds, 226 were sunk, including six destroyers and, I understand, two hospital ships. A further 19 destroyers were put out of action. The operation's success meant that over a quarter of a million trained and seasoned troops were available for duty who would otherwise be lost. It should not be forgotten, however, that the Navy's efforts would have been in vain had not the BEF been able to get the troops to the harbour and beaches to be evacuated, to extricate them from the long, narrow bridgehead. It depended partly on logistical skills but mostly on the ability of the rearguard to hold the German advance on the Belgian side of the border, at least ten miles from Dunkirk itself, for the week of the operation. (The French army did equally well on the western front.) Had both the Royal Navy and the Army not been successful in their operations it is doubtful whether the enemy could have been held at bay until the belated entry of the United States into the war made victory possible.

Postscript

I served in the 92nd Field Regiment, RA, TA in Scotland, Lancashire and Northern Ireland as sergeant artillery clerk until the spring of 1942, when the regiment sailed for the Far East. A few months later I was commissioned in the Royal Army Ordnance Corps and was engaged for the rest of the war in the storage and supply of ammunition.

The regiment served in India, Iraq and (as it then was) Persia. It took part with distinction in the invasion and conquest of Sicily and in the invasion of and advance through Italy, culminating in four gruelling months in the Anzio beach-head. It was then transferred to the Low Countries and Germany in the final stages of the war.

The war record of this Territorial regiment was of the highest order and I am proud to have been for a time a humble member of such a band of civilian soldiers.